Land and Taxation

*Both ground-rents and the ordinary rent of land are a
species of revenue which the owner, in many cases,
enjoys without any care or attention of his own. Though
a part of this revenue should be taken from him in order
to defray the expenses of the state, no discouragement
will thereby be given to any sort of industry. The annual
produce of the land and labour of society, the real
wealth and revenue of the great body of the people,
might be the same after such a tax as before. Ground-
rents, and the ordinary rent of land, are, therefore,
perhaps, the species of revenue which can best bear to
have a peculiar tax imposed upon them.*

- Adam Smith, *The Wealth of Nations* (1776), Bk II, Ch.2, Art.1

Other books in this series

The Corruption of Economics
Mason Gaffney and Fred Harrison
Hdbk ISBN 0 85683 160 3
Ppbk ISBN 0 85683 151 4

A Philosophy for a Fair Society
Michael Hudson, G.J. Miller and Kris Feder
Hdbk ISBN 0 85683 161 1
Ppbk ISBN 0 85683 159 X

Forthcoming

Land Speculation and the Business Cycle
Mason Gaffney and Fred Harrison (Editors)
ISBN 0 85683 152 2

Private Property and Public Finance
Ronald Banks and Kenneth Jupp (Editors)
ISBN 0 85683 155 7

Long Wave Business Cycles
Francis Smith
ISBN 0 85683 156 5

GEORGIST PARADIGM SERIES
Series Editor: Fred Harrison, MSc

Land and Taxation

Nicolaus Tideman, PhD
Editor

The Georgist Paradigm is a model of political economy that offers comprehensive solutions to the social and ecological problems of our age. At its heart is a set of principles on land rights and public finance which integrates economic efficiency and social justice.

Shepheard-Walwyn (Publishers) Ltd.

in association with

Centre for Incentive Taxation Ltd.

First published in 1994 by
Shepheard-Walwyn (Publishers) Ltd.,
26 Charing Cross Road (Suite 34),
London WC2H ODH

in association with

Centre for Incentive Taxation Ltd.,
177 Vauxhall Bridge Road,
London SW1V 1EU.
Tel: 071 834 4266 Fax: 071 834 4979

British Library Cataloguing in Publication Data

A catalogue record of this book
is available from the British Library.

Hdbk ISBN 0 85683 162 X
Ppbk ISBN 0 85683 153 0

Printed and bound in Great Britain by
BPC Wheatons, Exeter.

Contents

Prologue:
Rent-ability
Fred Harrison

U se-rights to land have been and remain the most important aspect of human culture. These rights have been at the heart of the social process from the beginning of *homo sapiens* as a distinct species. A sophisticated matrix of practices, which were formalised as customs, ensured a stable relationship between the foraging groups and their habitat. As economic activity became more complex, tenurial rights evolved in sympathetic harmony. This was necessary, to ensure a balance between the demands for consumption and the need to preserve a sustainable system within the niches of nature that human beings chose to occupy.

Then along came civilised men. They disturbed the traditional harmony, as Michael Hudson and I explain in *A Philosophy for a Fair Society*. Brushing aside the life-cycle imperatives of Mother Earth, they developed an exploitative system of land rights which had two broad effects. The social consequences were most immediately visible. The new approach wrecked the harmony of society, causing landlessness and poverty, which polarised into class conflict. The second effect was the over-exploitation of nature herself, such that life itself became unsustainable. Whole civilisations - between 10 to 30 of them, depending on how you classify a civilisation[1] - have fallen victim to ecological degradation.

In the past, the over-exploitation of nature was localised and therefore did not threaten either the biosphere or *homo sapiens*. That has changed. We now have the awesome capacity to wipe out our species as we poison the atmosphere on which we rely for life. Nature herself would recover; but too many species have become extinct for us to be complacent about our capacity to survive. This means that the most urgent policy issue facing mankind is the redefinition of our relationship with land. All the other economic and political issues are subordinate; in fact, most of them stem from this one issue, the resolution to which solves the secondary problems.

Our starting point is the era of confused capitalism. The industrial mode of production, when linked to the market, can yield untold material riches. There need not be material deprivation anywhere in the world. Why, then, does poverty abound? Well, thanks to some of the legacies of civilisation, we have become skilled at creating poverty. Poverty is not a voluntary condition. The social system has to work hard to create homelessness and hunger. In the world today, 1.1 billion people live in absolute poverty (with an income of under $1 a day); and the scale of poverty is increasing. Why, if capitalism is capable of providing everyone who wants to work with a decent standard of living, is poverty an intractable problem? Because, ultimately, when all the camouflage is pushed aside, we find that our system of property rights in land - more precisely, the way in which we distribute the benefits from land - distorts society in a way that prevents people from earning their wages.

The first step in the direction of achieving generalised prosperity is to retrieve an understanding of the importance of land in society. In the past 20 years, ecologists have successfully reminded us of our primordial dependence on nature. Social scientists now have to relocate the role of land within contemporary cultural realities. There is no point in fantasising about the nature of a New World in the future: we need to know how to facilitate a smooth transition from an imperfect capitalist society to whatever may flow from the application of rational social principles. This book is one of a series dedicated to explaining how the solution must be articulated first and foremost in terms of a reform of the system of taxation.

The rule of sub-optimality

For the past 250 years, a consistent theme in the economic literature has been the wisdom of a very specific approach to public finance: the need to pay for public services out of public value - that is, the socially-created rent of land. That history, from the French Physiocrats to the economists of today, is reviewed in this volume by Professor Tideman. Through the twists and turns of theorising, from the British classical economists to the

American neo-classical economists of the late 20th century, the important lesson remains unfaulted: the rent-as-public-revenue policy yields the optimum system for financing the public sphere of life.

It may seem surprising, then, that governments persistently ignore this rational policy. It is not for the want of complaints from the public about the chaotic state of public finances. Reasonable people know that their society needs a public sector, which has to be financed; nonetheless, they harbour a deep-seated resentment against taxation. Why? Because they intuitively sense that there is something fundamentally wrong with the way we raise revenue.

Perhaps the single most aggravating fact is the one that has been highlighted by C. Lowell Harriss, professor emeritus of economics at Columbia University who was for many years the Executive Director of the American Academy of Political Science. In a speech in which he described a switch away from taxes on wages and profits and onto the rent of land, he noted the importance of a direct correspondence between payments and benefits.

> Where taxes are involved the individual gets neither more nor less service if he or she pays more or less tax.[2]

This irks. We are used to paying freely as much as we want to pay for exactly what we want to receive. These are the transactions that we routinely perform every day in "the market". That option - of tailoring money paid to benefits received - is in the main not open to the citizen in relation to the purchase of public goods. An unmarried man pays high taxes to finance the education of someone else's children. A healthy person pays for someone else's medical needs. Pensioners pay for the welfare services available to young couples who have their future in front of them. And so on. Many people do not begrudge the asymmetry in tax-and-benefits policy; many people do.

Is there a resolution to this problem of the absence of a correspondence between benefits and payments? There is: the one in which public expenditure is primarily financed out of the rent of the land. There are three major benefits to this policy which are not associated with taxation.

(1) The payer's obligations are precisely related to the benefits he receives from the community. If you choose to occupy high-rent land, that

is because the benefits accruing to the site are considerable - easy access to a good school, close proximity to a park, the availability of public transport, and so on.

(2) The payer has the right to reduce his payments by moving from high-rent to low-rent land. Such a move results in a reduction of the services that are available in the new location; but that is a decision freely made by the citizen.

(3) The payer is relieved of what Dr. Harriss calls "the anti-progress taxes" on the income earned from labour or the interest received on the savings and investments made out of earned income.

Economic rent is the value of land and natural resources after deducting the rewards that must legitimately accrue to those who invest labour and capital in and on the land (buildings, fences, drainage, and so on). The professional valuer has little difficulty in estimating the net value - the economic rent of land. Deducting the value of undepreciated improvements to reveal the rent of land is an exercise routinely performed in the property market.

Since there is no administrative problem with identifying land-rent, why has this revenue not been treated as the appropriate base for public revenue? In fact, at the local level, it has been, and in some parts of the world it continues to be, a means of raising revenue for municipal governments. The policy was instituted in New Zealand and Australia in the 19th century. In Europe in the 20th century, the policy received extensive political support. In Britain, the constitutional crisis of 1909 was the direct result of the Liberal government's determination to levy a tax on the rent of land. While the proposal made it as far as the statute book, it got no further. It was blocked, first by the intervention of the First World War and then by the political opportunity presented to the Conservatives who represented the landlords.

Denmark was more successful. The policy was introduced as a result of demands from farmers. In the period after the second world war, several countries adopted the rent-as-public-revenue philosophy, including Taiwan and Jamaica. But the proportion of rent that was payable by landowners was insignificant (with the exception of Taiwan): too low to have much of an effect on the local economies, and with no beneficial macro-economic effect. Nevertheless, they provide useful opportunities to test the empirical character of the proposal that the rent of land provides benefits beyond the revenue that it can yield for the public coffers. One example is provided by the city of Pittsburgh, Pennsylvania.

In 1913, Pittsburgh decided to adopt a two-rate property tax (imposing a heavier rate on the assessed value of land than on the value of buildings). The empirical consequences were dramatically illustrated by what happened after the city's economic base was ravaged by the decline in the steel industry during the 1970s. In 1979, the city decided to widen the gap in the property tax. The tax rate on the assessed value of land was doubled from 4.95% to 9.75%, while the tax rate on buildings was frozen. There was a building boom. Investment flowed into the city in as dramatic a way as anyone could have hoped, leading to the public acclamation of the city as a fine example of urban renewal. The result, comparing Pittsburgh with 14 other mid-west cities that failed to take similar fiscal action, are revealed in Table 1.[3]

The rent-as-public-revenue policy does not generally receive fair dealing at the hands of scholars. They find it difficult to square the empirical evidence with the prejudices to which they have become acquainted by economic theory. Yet the message from more than a dozen Pennsylvania cities that have adopted a similar two-rate property tax is unmistakably clear,[4] and it reinforces the theoretical conclusions that have been drawn by Adam Smith, David Ricardo, John Stuart Mill and Henry George in the 19th century, through to the grudging - fleetingly stated - observations of some contemporary economists.

Why, then, if rent is the superior source of public revenue, is it not treated with sympathy in the corridors of power? There are a variety of reasons.

In the United States, landowners donate substantial sums of money to the campaign funds of compliant politicians. Historically, this facilitated a switch in taxation onto consumption and production, which is where the vested interests now intend it to remain. The real estate sector suffers terribly from the cyclical booms and slumps that result from intense speculation in the land market, but memories are short and the major landowners - the ones who speculate over the long term - are able to ride out the turmoil. The principal losers are the suckers who enter the land market when prices are near the insupportable peak; and also, of course, the generality of citizens, whose social and economic aspirations are distressingly

Table 1

**15 midwest cities
before and after Pittsburgh's major land tax increase.
Average annual value of building permits.**

Constant 1982 dollars: millions

	1960-79	**1980-89**	**% change**
PITTSBURGH	181.7	309.7	70.4
Akron	134.0	87.9	-34.4
Allentown	48.1	28.8	-40.4
Buffalo	93.7	82.9	-11.5
Canton	40.2	24.2	-39.7
Cincinnati	318.2	231.5	-27.2
Cleveland	329.5	224.5	-31.8
Columbus	456.5	527.0	15.4
Dayton	107.7	92.2	-14.4
Detroit	368.8	277.7	-24.7
Erie	48.3	22.7	-52.9
Rochester	118.7	82.4	-30.5
Syracuse	94.5	53.6	-43.2
Toledo	138.3	93.4	-32.4
Youngstown	33.6	11.1	-66.9
15-CITY AVERAGE	167.5	143.3	-14.4

SOURCE: Gates and Schwab (1992), Table 3.

terminated by the bouts of unemployment that necessarily follow speculation in future increases in the rent of land. In Britain, the constraints on public policy imposed by the landowning interests are more subtly incorporated into the political process, but with a similar result.

It would be incorrect to limit the explanation to a conspiracy of landowners, however, for successive Labour governments in postwar Britain enjoyed the freedom to implement legislation designed to capture at least a part of the value that is created by the community. The failure of these laws had less to do with retribution from the landowning class, and - as Vic Blundell explains in his contribution to this volume - more to do with the clumsy drafting of the structure of the taxes themselves. That clumsiness, however, was not wilful. It was, as we shall see, the result of confusion injected into economics.

The theory of poverty

Few countries in the world can claim that their finances are not in a mess.

Governments cannot keep abreast of the demands made upon them for more money: social problems keep escalating beyond the capacity to finance the social obligations that are deemed to be necessary for their solution.

The impact of the present structure of taxation on the fabric of society has not yet been evaluated. That influence extends from the criminalisation of people who simply want to be free to earn a decent living, to the creation of a state of dependency as the hold of the bureaucracy and the tax-avoidance professionals is deepened in people's private affairs.

If there is one subject that unites practically everyone, today, it is hostility to taxation. This hostility is not based on irrationality; people know that society needs the resources to meet communal obligations. But there is something that rankles them about the tax system. Despite all the talk of fairness with which fiscal policy is hedged, citizens intuitively believe that there is something fundamentally wrong with the system of public finance. Their instincts are correct. Public finance is based on principles of arbitrariness and oppression. That is why citizens would just as soon avoid paying taxes if they can get away with it; and many of them do just that, with the "black" (i.e., criminal - because tax-evading) economy in Britain officially estimated to be around £40 billion.

There can be no doubt that society is in urgent need of reform of the system of public finance. The authors of this book are united by the vision of what could be achieved by an enlightened policy: fairness in the payments to the community; a heightened level of personal prosperity; and a liberation of the community of a kind that would constitute a social renaissance. Is this pie-in-the-sky? There is one approach to public finance that could deliver this result. There is no secret about the policy: it is the most ancient of approaches to paying for the services that are collectively required by the community. The policy focuses on the surplus income generated by the economy, the economic rent of land.

Rent can be measured very precisely. It is what is left over, after paying the labour and capital costs of production in a competitive market. If, on a particular site, the weekly costs of producing a product for sale was £4,500 - paying all wages, interest on bank loans, a "profit" for the owner of the building and equipment on which the article was manufactured; and if the price of the product in the marketplace yielded a weekly revenue of £5,000, then the economic rent of the site, in its bare condition, is £500. That is the sum that would be claimed by the owner of the land on which the enterprise was built. And if people decided, through the democratic process, to restructure the tax system in favour of revenue from the economic rent of land - and untaxing their wages and profits - they would be creating the optimum conditions for the welfare of both the private and public sectors.

During the late 18th and 19th centuries, the classical economists proved theoretically that our ancestors, from tribal peoples to the folk of the archaic and classical civilisations right through to the Anglo-Saxons and their Norman conquerors, were correct: the most efficient way to raise public revenue was from the surplus generated by activity on land.

In the 1880s the case was convincingly restated by Henry George, so why, over the past 100 years, have governments avoided this reform? Before reflecting on the role of economists in the distortion of economic policy, we first need to confront the question of whether we can, indeed, take for granted, that the Georgist approach to taxation would deliver the benefits we want. Let us reflect on the problem of poverty.

Henry George saw that, if people were not taxed on their wages and the returns to their capital, there would be no involuntary unemployment; and incomes would be good enough for everyone, such that poverty would be a historical curiosity. The legitimate financial needs of the community, he argued, would be adequately catered for out of the economic rent of land; a policy that was dubbed "the Single Tax".

His book, *Progress and Poverty*, when it was published in 1879, explained the mechanisms by which this result would be achieved. People throughout the world, having turned the book into the most popular text on economics ever to be published, decided that they, too, accepted the blindingly obvious.[5] So Henry George had to be stopped. Before considering one way in which this was accomplished, let us ask the question: were the millions of people who accepted George's analysis - throughout America, the British Isles, down to the Antipodes, they bought his book and packed his public meetings - wrong? Was he misleading them, in arguing that he had perceived the way to abolish poverty through a reform of the tax system?

Conventional economists believe him to be wrong, but can we respect their conclusion? Unlike Henry George, they do not provide an alternative theory of poverty. Furthermore, they decline to engage his propositions in debate. They dismiss his case on the basis of assertion rather than rigorous argument. That may explain, of course, why the world continues to suffer from an escalation in poverty, despite the break through the barriers that once obstructed us from a state of generalised material prosperity.

To provide the reader with an overview of the controversy we shall recall the work of Joseph Schumpeter (1883-1950), a finance minister in Austria after the first world war before becoming a professor of economics in Bonn, from whence he moved to Harvard in 1932.

In his *History of Economic Analysis*, Schumpeter stressed that, although self-taught, Henry George *was* an economist. Indeed, Schumpeter notes that the way in which George acquired his knowledge was to his advantage. He had held a variety of jobs before finally settling down as a journalist in San Francisco, acquiring his economic knowledge from real life rather than by academic training.

Schumpeter characterises the Single Tax as a "panacea". Nonetheless, Henry George "was careful to frame his 'remedy' in such a manner as to cause the minimum injury to the efficiency of the private-enterprise economy".[6] On what basis was the proposal denigrated as a panacea? Well, wrote Schumpeter, the policy was "vitiated by association with the untenable theory that the phenomenon of poverty is entirely due to the absorption of all surpluses by the rent of land". He then proceeds to concede that George's fiscal proposal "is not *economically* unsound" (Schumpeter's emphasis). The problem, in his view, related to one specific issue: the proposal "involves an unwarranted optimism concerning the yield of such a tax".

Here we have one of the crunch tests. Schumpeter, like all the other major economists of the 20th century, transgressed the basic principles of science. He resorted to assertion - w ithout theoretical discourse, let alone reference to empirical evidence - to claim that the rent of land would not provide sufficient revenue to finance the needs of the modern nation.

> In any case, it should not be put down as nonsense. If Ricardo's vision of economic evolution had been correct, it would even have been obvious wisdom. And obvious wisdom is in fact what George said in *Progress and Poverty* (Ch.1, Book IX) about the economic effects to be expected from a removal of fiscal burdens - if such a removal were feasible.[7]

In his discussion, Schumpeter lists what he postulates as the two problems with the tax policy that is the only radical alternative available to society. First, the proposal is disgraced by its association with the claim about the origins of poverty. Second, that land-rent constitutes an insufficient tax base for modern needs.

The books in this series on the Georgist paradigm re-examine the proposition that the major social problems would be resolved by the reform of the tax system along the lines prescribed by, among others, Henry George. The authors have compared the alternatives and cannot find serious competitors for the hypotheses that flow from the Georgist paradigm. Here, we can only consider the tantalising issues that touch on Schumpeter's two concerns.

On poverty: as Schumpeter noted, Henry George's economic analysis was so transparently clear that millions of citizens accepted the truth of what he wrote. Were they wrong? It is possible, of course. But among those readers was a nuclear physicist, Albert Einstein. In a letter dated October 8, 1931, Einstein wrote:

> I read the largest part of the book by Henry George with extraordinary

interest, and I believe that in the main points the book takes a stand which cannot be fought, especially as far as the cause of poverty is concerned.[8]

Would it not be extraordinary for a mind such as Einstein's to draw such an emphatic conclusion on poverty, if he was in any way dubious about the analysis? Einstein concluded that, if we wanted to deal with poverty, we had to pursue the line of reasoning displayed in *Progress and Poverty*.

This is a view shared by Dr. Fred Foldvary, who in his contribution to this volume re-examines the theory of wages. He finds that progress towards a solution on poverty is contingent on policy initiatives that must include a unique combination of reforms to the structure of both public finance and the markets, reforms that flow from the principles of the Georgist paradigm. Dr. Foldvary, while substantially agreeing with Schumpeter's analysis of how other theorists treated wages, was disappointed to find that Schumpeter afforded Henry George's theory of wages an incomplete treatment compared with the weight he gave to other economists.

What of Schumpeter's second concern - the revenue-yielding capacity of land? Was it really insufficient to meet the needs of the nation? Schumpeter's view is taken as axiomatic by his colleagues, the academic economists who purport to study these matters. Typical of this school of economic analysis is the work by two prominent British economists, John Kay and Mervyn King. In referring to Henry George, they claim that it is "apparent" that "the total of economic rents, of all kinds, is not now a sufficiently large proportion of national income for this to be a practicable means of obtaining the resources needed to finance a modern State".[9] This conclusion, while "apparent" to conventional economists, is not correct.

The measurable rental value of Britain's land and natural resources has been calculated at well over 20% of the nation's income,[10] including the rent that must be imputed to owner-occupiers who do not actually receive rent as a cash income (the taxation of imputed income is discussed below). This is a handsome proportion of government revenue, by any standard. Typically, however, as with most economists who write in their textbooks about the taxable capacity of land, Kay and King do not offer a shred of evidence for dismissing the size of the economic rent in the modern economy.

The one economist who has spent his lifetime reflecting on the question, however, draws a different conclusion. Mason Gaffney is a professor of economics at the University of California. In his view, the economic rent of *a tax-free society* is around 40%.[11] This is sufficient to meet the needs of the most avaricious of modern States! There is evidently a scholarly dispute here that needs to be authoritatively resolved if public policy is to be reformed from an enlightened perspective. That debate will not be conducted until we retrieve the concept of land from the intellectual cupboard into which the neo-classical economists worked strenuously to lock it a century ago. Prof. Gaffney, in his contribution to this volume, takes this process of rehabilitation a step forward by prising open the door to that cupboard: he re-educates his colleagues on the distinctive qualities of land as a factor of production. Land cannot be sensibly analysed as if it were just a sub-category of "capital"; the relegation of land to the sidelines has done more than anything else to lead economists up the policy *cul-de-sacs*, wherein confusion was caused to the profession and bewildering pain to the citizens.

Empirical tests will prove that Henry George was correct. We confidently draw that conclusion because the reforms that he commended can be located in a theoretical tradition that has not yet been falsified, despite the best endeavours of the neo-classical economists. But why, then, has George's primary reform, to the system of public finance, not yet been executed?

When it became clear that Henry George was serious; that he was intruding into the politics of his era - in Britain and Ireland and Australia; in China (via the nationalist leader Sun Yat-sen) and in Russia (via Leo Tolstoy); that he was determined to push for fiscal reform in an epoch-making campaign, the historic logic of his arguments had to be neutralised. How this was accomplished by the neo-classical economists, at the turn into the 20th century, is the subject of an investigation into intellectual dishonesty by Professor Gaffney.[12] The neo-classicals set about obliterating the distinctive features of the concept of economic rent. This, in turn, succeeded in obscuring the unique characteristics of a policy that had enjoyed a tradition measured by the millenia.

Economists, by convoluting their concepts, were able to pretend that the rent of land was not, after all, something special. That was convenient for those who had not the slightest desire to publicise the virtues of the most efficient system of public finance. How was this accomplished? The neo-classicals set about proving that both labour and capital could also earn rent! So why, in that case, single out land as the unique source of public revenue?

Schumpeter did not approve of some of the treatments that had been accorded to the concept of economic rent. He noted "a tendency to harness the concept of rent into the service of entirely different purposes" which, *inter alia*, lead to "waverings, haziness and spurious issues".[13] Distinguished economists participated in the extension of the definition of rent, "though, in my opinion, this only served to expose its emptiness".

If, now, a nation wishes to rebase its affairs on a rational, efficient system framed by justice, it will have to treat the rent of land as something special. But that will not happen if economists are allowed to continue to cloud the issues that are at stake. If the prejudices and practises of 800 years are to be corrected - that is how long it took for the Norman aristocrats and their heirs to privatise the public revenue in Britain[14] - it will first be necessary to engage in a democratic debate. That process will be energetically resisted by the vested interests that continue to wield the ultimate power in society; but for the will of the majority to express itself effectively the issues will have to be clarified once again, through the process of demystification.

As a start, it is necessary to examine what conventional economists mean when they say that labour and capital also earn rent; for then we might be better able to decide whether such a claim is a good reason for not singling out land as the unique base for the optimum system of public finance. We cannot leave the concept of optimum taxation to economists, for they are not willing to devote sufficient time or space to the idea, as some of them, at least, are willing to acknowledge.[15]

The mystification of rent

We can take as an example the work of John Kay of the London Business School and Mervyn King, formerly a professor of economics at the London School of Economics, who is now Chief Economist at the Bank of England. Their treatment of the tax system, which has passed through five editions, is singled out for no special reason. It fairly represents the teaching manuals on public finance that are recommended to students. *The British Tax System* derives much of its popularity from the fact that it is a text used by the Open University. This means it exercises influence on the way that mature students, members of the public who sit in judgment on the record of politicians when the time comes to elect a new government, think about public finance.

In Chapter 12, we are told that economic rent has a specific technical meaning in economics. The point is illustrated in this way:

> If a singer earns £100,000 a year, and his next best employment would be as a barber at £5,000 per year, then he is obtaining economic rent of £95,000.[16]

Without his exceptional voice, the singer would be clipping locks for the lesser sum and using his voice for the tips his amused customers might be willing to add to his wages. Kay and King draw two conclusions from their illustration:

(i) "...rent is the result of the scarcity of particular factors of production. If all barbers would make equally good singers, then the earnings of singers would be bid down to the earnings of barbers, and no rent would be derived."

(ii) "...the rent could be taxed, or otherwise reduced, without any economic distortion resulting. So long as our singer nets more than £5,000 per year, he will continue his present occupation and stay out of the barber's shop."

Why extend the concept of rent to someone's wages? Schumpeter offered one explanation:

> It constitutes in fact a typical instance of unnecessary confusion being created for no better reason than a preference for terms that, like rent, have acquired derogatory associations. If it were not for this, it would be readily recognized that 'surplus' does all that is needed and that the term 'rent,' in this connection, is redundant.[17]

Whatever the motive for causing confusion, of one thing we can be sure: for those who opposed the policy of rent-as-public-revenue, muddying the theoretical waters was a godsend. For the new theoretical formulation could be - and was - used to deny the wisdom of changing back to the system in which people's wages and profits were privatised (that is, untaxed) in line with a switch to rent-revenue.

But if we dissect the differences in the incomes going to land, on the one hand, and labour and capital, on the other, we accumulate such a list of differences that it becomes absurd to try and lock the incomes of all three factors of production into single categories; an absurdity that distorts democratic debate and public policy. I shall briefly review the differences under four headings:

- The nature of rent
- Social justice
- Enforceability
- Efficiency

(1) The nature of rent

Is rent the result of scarcity? Scarcity can apply in any of the markets. Scientists with special skills might suddenly become scarce; those willing to provide their services would be able to claim a premium over the wages of their colleagues. Some would say: "Lucky for them!" Conventional economists would claim that the difference was economic rent. Similarly in the capital markets. For a time, an entrepreneur might have an advantage which he could translate into a rate of return above what his capital would earn in other uses: again, the conventional economist would claim that capital was receiving income that was composed of both interest and rent. So why make a fuss about the distinctive qualities of the income received by land?

One difference is to be uncovered by identifying the way in which the value accrued to the factor of production that is in scarce supply. The scientist had to acquire the skill which - luckily for him - turns out to be scarce. His earning capacity is therefore raised above the level of the wage that he would otherwise have earned as a run-of-the-mill scientist. Similarly with capital: the entrepreneur who discovered he could command a premium on top of the average rate of interest had to have undertaken (or be willing to undertake) the investment, in the first place, thereby placing his capital at an advantage. In both cases, the income is actively earned by those who command the labour and capital.

Now, turning to land, ask the question: if a piece of land can command rent, who created that value? It is not sufficient to say, as Kay and King contentedly do, that scarcity, *per se*, results in rent.

We do not make land; therefore, its supply is fixed, and by definition it is scarce. But what are people paying for, when they seek to occupy a site?

It is not scarcity, by itself, that fixes the price: they can go and live on the outer rims of Siberia and pay no rent whatsoever.

Rent is the price people are willing to pay for the benefits they know they would receive from the occupation of particular sites. The rent of land is the one figure that sums up the value of these kinds of services:

• availability of public transport and refuse collection;

• access to hospitals and schools;

• intangible qualities that are accorded to a neighbourhood as a result of levels of crime and sociability;

• proximity to shops and recreation amenities, and so on.

The value of these services to people varies according to a variety of considerations: age (old folk place a premium on the ready access to doctors); aesthetics (some people are willing to pay over-the-odds for a "green" view from their sitting room window); marital status (young families need convenient access to schools); income levels (public transport is more important to those who cannot afford to own a car, or who do not wish to commute long distances on overcrowded roads); and so on. Some of these considerations are subjective, but they pass through a process of "objectification" through the medium of the marketplace. By this, I mean that subjective preferences are evened out by the pricing mechanism - the amount of money one person is willing to offer, as rent, relative to the amount that others are willing to offer for the access to particular sites that give them access to the amenities that they require.

Now we see the unique nature of rent. It is the sum of the value placed by people on the availability of public services and the overall quality of "the community". The finite supply of land becomes a way of rationing access to services in particular places. This is why people are obliged to compete for the right of access to sites: the occupation of the sites gives them access to the services that are available in the community of their choice. The amount of rent they are willing to pay is their public declaration of the value they place on the services to which they want access. But unlike the worker or the capitalist, who finds himself in the fortunate position of being able to claim extraordinary wages or super-profits in return for services rendered, the services of land are not provided by the owner of the land.

The distinctions in the payments made to land, labour and capital, then, can be summarised in terms of the benefits principle. If you pay the scientist for his special skill, you pay the person who provides the service. Similarly, if you pay over-the-odds to a capitalist for the use of his unique equipment, you pay the person who provides the service, scarce or otherwise. But under our system of property rights, when you pay rent for the use of land you pay someone who does not provide the services that are accessible to the site. This is a qualitative difference that must not be obliterated by the economist's bland assertion that economic rent is the result of scarcity.

(2) Social justice

Conventional economists, while priding themselves in the oft-repeated claim that they are "positive" scientists - that they forgo the normative approach to economics based on subjective values - nonetheless spend a great deal of their time balancing the "trade-offs" between efficiency and equity considerations. But their concepts of equity are largely brought to bear in a subjective manner. They presume to *know* positively what people regard as fair, so they devote enormous time and space to drawing economic conclusions based on their perception of social justice.[18]

People do have a powerful sense of justice. They do wish their society to be governed by the rules that they would collectively agree were fair. And I believe that there is little ambiguity about the principle that would shape their concept of a fair system of public finance. My assertion, which I would be happy to put to the democratic test - as it was, successfully, in Britain, in the "People's Budget" controversy of 1909, relates to the rules that would govern fairness in public finance. These are twofold. First, people ought to pay for what they receive. Second, people ought not to be paid for services that are rendered or financed by others.

In terms of public finance, this means that public services ought to be financed by the value that it creates - the economic rent of land. Rent is the payment for services that are largely provided by the public; and that value ought not (in all fairness) to be pocketed by people who do not pay for, or provide, those services. In the non-jargon language of Alfred Marshall (1842-1924), who straddled the classical with the post-classical period of economics:

> Looking forward rather than backwards, and not concerning ourselves
> with the equity and the proper limits of the present private property in land,

we see that that part of the national dividend which goes as earnings of land is a surplus in a sense in which the earnings from other agents are not a surplus.[19]

And, to drum home the uniqueness of the income attributed to land, Marshall added:

> ...there is this difference between land and other agents of production, that from a social point of view land yields a permanent surplus, while perishable things made by man do not.[19]

If the rent of land and natural resources is a "surplus", in the way that the earnings of labour and capital are not, then the layman, in all conscience, is not inclined to approve of any one person, or class of persons, appropriating that income. Are they not likely to say that this value therefore ought to be devoted to the collective needs of the community, to finance the services that create the value in the first place?

(3) Enforceability

We now turn to the question of enforcing the collection of economic rent. Here, again, we see that there is a world of difference between the income of land and the income received by labour and capital.

Let us return to the case of the singer whose income is, in large measure, rent, according to Kay and King. What if the government were to tell the singer: "We intend to take 5% of your rental income as tax"? We can reasonably expect the singer to pay up, without fuss. But what if the government were to say: "You have not *earned* that £95,000, for you would willingly work as a singer for £5,000 - the sum you would otherwise earn as a barber. We shall therefore impose an income tax at the rate of 95% on your income"? In that case, the singer has two options:

(i) He could pay, and his fans would hope that he would not so grind his teeth in anger as to affect his singing; or

(ii) He could refuse to sing; in which case, he would work as a barber for £5,000, and his fans would be deprived of their entertainment.

What could the government do about the impertinence of strategy (ii)? Could it coerce the barber to return to singing in order to extract economic rent from him? Hardly. Recall the case of the Beatles. Without their role as entertainers, John, Paul, George and Ringo would not have had the capacity to earn the millions of pounds that they commanded for just one record. When they decided to break up the partnership, impresarios offered fortunes to try and entice them into singing in harmony once again: but the ex-Beatles could not be tempted. What chance, then, would the government have had of forcing John, Paul, George and Ringo back on stage just to earn additional money to pay to the taxman?

The costs of enforceability - of reaping the so-called economic rent of wages - are daunting. In fact, they are ultimately impossible, and the costs are not restricted solely to economic considerations. The Soviet Union had a device for persuading reluctant workers: they were sent to Siberia and told that they would be released when their job of work was completed (a fate that befell many nuclear physicists). That approach to tax enforcement is not available in a free society, although a modified variant of it is occasionally tried. An example from Norway is revealing.

In 1993, the Norwegian government decided that it would try to squeeze more money - most of it "rent" - out of artists. A law was passed that ordered artists to pay tax on the value of all works that were not sold more than one year after production. The artists protested. They claimed that it could take anything up to 30 years to sell a painting (Van Gogh died in poverty). On April 12, 1994, about 500 artists marched on the Storting (parliament). They expressed their feelings by destroying their works of art with axes and knives. So far as one knows, there are no colonies inside Norway's arctic circle where artists turn out masterpieces to meet the "rental" claims of the government.

Now apply the problem to land. If the government were to claim that occupiers were obliged to pay for the services they received, we find ourselves dealing with a wholly different order of things. First, the users are merely being asked to pay for the services that they wish to receive. Second, the payment is the amount that they (and not the government) declare to be the value of the services that they want to receive. Third, the enforcement costs are minimal.

Expanding on this latter point, we can see that, unlike labour or capital (which are mobile and can flee across jurisdictional boundaries), land cannot be transported to tax havens. So what can the government do, if an occupier refuses to pay the annual rent of his land for the benefit of the services he receives from the occupation of his site? Here are two possibilities:

(i) The government could try to deny the occupier access to public services. This is not a viable option. The problems can be perceived at two levels.

Direct action would have to be taken against the occupier to deal with one set of amenities that are uniquely associated with particular sites. But how do you stop the occupier of land walking down the road and boarding a train at the nearest subway station? Or of continuing to enjoy the scenery from his land - if that was a primary reason for obtaining possession of the site in the first place? Or of walking his dog in the nearest park? In principle, you could bar him from the enjoyment of all these amenities, but the problem of enforcement would be taxing, to say the least.

The second group of considerations relate to the general factors that give value to land. Territorial defence is the bedrock of economic rent. To see how this works, recall how, during periods of geopolitical instability, money flows into the United States. Why? Because that country is perceived to be "stable". The stability is associated with the defencibility of the realm. Can - would - a government inform a recalcitrant occupier of land who refuses to pay for public services that his piece of land will not be defended by the armed might of the State? Hardly! The sovereign nation would refuse to yield its primary function: territorial defence.

(ii) Distraint is the alternative to denying public services to the occupier of land who refuses to pay for them. This ultimate sanction, which is routinely employed by landlords against tenants who fail to pay rent, involves the courts; the services of a policeman are secured to remove the occupier from the land. The land can then be made available to someone who is willing to pay for the services provided by the community.

The second option is a viable one, in the way that the use of coercion on people to secure their "rent" of wages is not.

This discussion has served to highlight further the differences between labour and capital, on the one hand, and land, on the other. If a talented scientist turned himself into a hermit, rather than pay rent-of-ability to the government, it would be possible to increase the supply of his skills by the process of education. This is not the case with land: it is in fixed supply.[20] The community can "live with" the withdrawal of the services of labour, but it cannot - without severe cost - tolerate the withdrawal of the services of land.

(4) Efficiency

Efficiency is an important criterion for judging the acceptability of particular taxes. We shall focus on just one issue, and that comes back to the question of who, ultimately, actually pays.

With labour and capital, the general rule is that taxes on wages and profits are passed on to consumers in the form of higher prices. There are exceptions, depending on the degree of mobility of labour, in particular (capital is almost perfectly mobile). If an employee cannot easily move to another taxing jurisdiction, a new tax will reduce his net wage. With land, however, the obligation to pay rent to the community ultimately falls exclusively on whoever derives the benefits of occupation.

The conclusion that landowners cannot pass on the "tax" on rent, in the form of higher rents, has been attested by nearly all the major economists of the past two centuries. The explanation for this is simple enough. As we have seen, the obligation to pay rent can be enforced; and the enforcement would not reduce the supply of land.

The fixity of the supply of land has been acknowledged ever since Adam Smith turned economics into a social science; it is not, as the late Professor Prest suggested,[21] something laboured as "an element of incontrovertible truth by the inveterate promoters of land taxation". Prest argued that there were cases where the elasticity in the supply of land was not zero.[22] His examples, involving the switch of land between different uses within or between the urban and rural sectors, do not undermine the time-honoured conclusion that the obligation to pay part or all of the rent of land or natural resources to the community does not result in a rise in the rent of land; and does not distort the allocation of resources between competing uses.

Prest's attempt to qualify the theory of rent-as-public-revenue[23] has no force, if we are talking about applying a uniform rate of payment on market-based rents, and where the obligation to pay is applied to all land throughout the nation in its different uses. His discussion of how the tax itself might distort the supply of land is of little interest to us, here; for it is drawn from postwar British experience, and is therefore based on policies that were doomed to failure from the outset, as Vic Blundell explains.

The remedy for land speculation
The value of the fiscal policy generated by the Georgist paradigm is not
restricted to its revenue-raising characteristics. We explain, in another
volume, that land speculation is the primary cause of the business cycle.
Henry George argued that the only effective way to remove the propensity
to speculate in land is to re-socialise the social revenue, while reprivatising
the private revenue. This result could not be achieved, however - in other
words, the business cycle could not be smoothed out - if the Georgist
paradigm discriminated between owner-occupied land and land that is
leased by tenants who pay rent to landlords. Everyone ought to pay for the
benefits that are derived from the possession of land, and this is achieved
by imputing rental income to the owner-occupier, an income that ought then
to be paid to the Treasury to finance the benefits received by the owner-
occupier. How that proposal is obstructed is fascinating; and once again,
it is the neo-classical theory that is employed to confuse the policy-makers.

    One reason that is advanced for rejecting this policy is derived from the
belief that the same principle would have to be applied to the imputed
income from other assets.[24] Does that not sound fair? In fact, this is a
nonsense argument; but we will have to treat it seriously, even if only
because it further exposes the confusions injected into economics by the
neo-classical school.

    The argument is given short-shrift by tax economist William Musgrave,
who rebuts it in terms of feasibility.

> The answer again is that in principle all imputed income (including even
> income from cash-holding) should be taxed, but that it is not a feasible
> procedure. Taxation of imputed rent, on the other hand, is feasible. The
> inequity between owners and renters, which results from the present
> practice of deducting mortgage interest while not taxing imputed rent, is
> unfair, especially at the lower end of the income scale, and could be
> improved even by a rough approximation of imputed rent.[25]

    In fact, the feasibility argument is a minor feature of the case for rejecting
the claim that, if you tax the "income" that is notionally received by
someone who owns land, to be consistent you also have to tax the income
that might be imputed to, say, the ownership of an asset like a 10-ton lorry.
Identifying and "taxing" the imputed rent of privately-owned land is

practical, but a far more powerful case exists for treating the rent of land as special for fiscal purposes.

To place the current political problem of public finance in its context, I shall focus on two differences between the income-receiving characteristics of land, on the one hand, and, say, the fully operational 10-ton lorry, which the eccentric owner chooses to display in his garden, with no intention of hauling goods.

Both the land and the lorry can earn income. The landowner can rent out his site; the lorry owner could haul goods and charge for the use of his vehicle. Assume that the two owners choose to withhold their assets from commercial use. In terms of taxation, why should we differentiate between them? Let us start by considering the issue of value.

A team of people produced the lorry. They assembled the raw materials, operated the machinery, marketed the product. The purchaser covered, in full, the cost of production: he owes nothing to anyone for the right to claim title to the lorry. Why, if he chooses not to earn income from his asset, should he be penalised by the State, through the taxation of the income that could be imputed to the asset (that is, the income that the lorry would generate if it were used to haul goods)?

Now reflect on the characteristics of a piece of raw land. It has a value: that value is not the measure of the cost of production, for there is no such cost. The value is the rent that the owner imputes to his land. On what basis does he impute rental value? The swiftest answer is that the owner examines the rents paid "in the market" for comparable sites, and that is what he charges for his site. But that begs the question: of what does rent comprise? If the owner were obliged to offer a breakdown of the calculation, this is what he would say.

First, it is necessary to estimate the total value of the services - provided by public agencies, and all the citizens who comprise the community - that accrue to the occupant of the site. But the rent that the owner can charge does not comprise the whole of this value; for the prospective occupant knows that he faces some charges (such as taxes and user fees). These financial obligations have to be deducted from the total value of the benefits that accrue to the site. The landowner then exacts the difference from anyone who wishes to occupy his site.

Now we have a problem. Rent is the cash measure of the services provided to each and every site. If I buy a piece of land, under the present law on tenure and taxation, I pay a price that is the annual rent that is capitalised by the previous owner into a selling price. In other words, the previous owner will not relinquish title to the land unless he is paid the rent that expresses the value that is expected to accrue to the land over the next 10 or 20 years. Now we see the problem. Over the next 10 or 20 years, the public has to finance the provision of the services that give rental value to that piece of land: garbage disposal, sewer works, road maintenance, the provision of parks, schools and mass transit systems.

So, from my viewpoint as the landowner: I could choose not to use my land, but the services still have to be financed. I *could* use the land, and derive the benefit of the publicly-provided services...I *do* deny other people access to those services, by refusing to let them use my land...I *will* eventually capitalise the rental value of those services into a selling price, and charge someone else for the privilege of occupying my site...

From the social viewpoint: the services have to be provided, whether an individual site-owner properly uses his land or not. The fire brigade and the police force have to be on stand-by, in case the landowner calls them into action. The roads that border the site have to be maintained, even if the owner keeps the land padlocked. There is no escaping the financing of those services that make a community what it is - a community in which it is worth living.

Conclusion: I, the landowner, continue to be indebted to the community for providing the services that make the occupation of my site attractive. In terms of *the benefits principle*, I, the landowner, continue to derive value from the community - through my ownership of the site - even if I do not put the site to use. Am I not under an obligation to pay for those services?

The answer, in all conscience, is "Yes!" But now we arrive at a major moral problem. It is a problem that is ignored by politicians, which is why we necessarily cannot have good government. I, the owner, can sell my land at a price that reflects the cost of publicly-provided services, a cost that others - taxpayers, most of them not the owners of land - therefore have to meet out of the wages and profits that they earn.

Now consider how the new owner of the site - who chooses not to put the land to income-yielding use - would feel, if he were required to finance the services that accrue to his site. He has already paid for those services in the form of the money he handed over to the previous owner. Consternation! Naturally, the new owner does not wish to pay twice for the benefit of receiving the same services. And if the government takes the imputed rent of the land to pay for those services, the owner is, indeed, being made to pay twice over: on the first occasion, he paid the previous landowner (did *he* have the moral right to charge for services funded by the community?); and the second time, now, as the government "taxes" the rental value of the site to pay for the services.

There is a clear injustice here. If a theatre owner told his patrons that, as the price of admission, they would have to pay double the price of a seat, he would be left with an empty auditorium! If a car-maker told his customers that, just for the hell of it, they would be charged double the costs of production - similarly, the customers would wither away! So why should the occupant of a site, who has paid the previous owner the price of the public services he is to receive, then be told that he now has to pay the public agencies for the services that he wants to receive?

This is an awesome social problem, but it is not one that ought to be ignored. For an equivalent injustice is being perpetrated on taxpayers, and especially those taxpayers who are also rent-paying tenants. Under the present principles of public finance, they pay more for public services than the benefits that they receive. This double-dealing is a time-honoured one, of course, but is not acceptable for all that. This is what happens. Taxpayers ought to receive in benefits a value that equals their contributions to the public exchequer, plus what they pay in user charges (the price of a ticket for travelling on public transport, for example). In fact, they do not get a fair deal. For part of the aggregate value of their payments is sumped off in the form of the rent of land which is pocketed by landowners.

We now turn to the second difference. The lorry owner is not depriving anyone of a job, or an improvement in his lifestyle, just because he chooses not to use his lorry. There are many more identical lorries to be bought and hired where his came from! The more the lorries parked idly in people's gardens, the faster the conveyor belt turning out lorries. No-one's goods need go unhauled; and competition among haulage firms ensures that the cost of operating the lorry is brought down to the minimum level consistent with making it worthwhile to operate the vehicle.

But what happens if the landowner withdraws his land from use? It cannot be replaced: no-one makes land. The total supply of land is reduced by one site. Multiply the decision to keep the land idle, and what happens? Rents rise, because of the increase in the demand for those sites that remain in use; and, under the present rules of the economic game, the prospects are good that this will encourage landowners to withdraw additional land in the expectation of speculatively-high capital gains in the future. Aggregate supply falls rapidly, and there is a macro-economic impact: as the rent of land is artificially increased, employment prospects and living standards are reduced.

In purely economic terms, then, there is no good reason for treating land as the equal of other assets. Land and capital may be substituted for each other, in certain circumstances, but that is not the same as saying that they should be treated as identical for purposes of public revenue. The fatuous argument of the kind addressed by Professor Musgrave is good for occupying time in the classroom; unfortunately, it serves to confuse the politicians, and therefore contributes to the failure of public policy.

In this brief analysis we have identified the cause of the mess of the nation-state. Wage- and profit-earners are forced to pay for public services, the net economic benefits of which are transformed into the rent that is appropriated by landowners. How did this confusion of policy come about? Historically, it was engineered by the privatisation of public revenue; a social injustice that was then preserved by conceptual trickery, by the device of eradicating the distinctive qualities of land and capital.

When a tax isn't a tax

In the foregoing section I qualified the word tax within quotation marks when I referred to fiscal obligations imposed on the recipients of economic rent. This is because such a payment, while it is traditionally referred to as "land value taxation" in the literature, is not, in fact, a tax.

A tax is an arbitrarily fixed levy on people's incomes, a payment that is not precisely tailored to the benefits that the individual taxpayer receives. When people pay tax on their earned incomes, for example, they may, or may not, wish to use the health service on which their taxes are spent; some people pay both taxes and the health insurance premiums that give them access to private medicine. A childless taxpayer's money is partly spent on public education. Part of the income of a tax-paying philistine - who would never dream of visiting an opera house - is devoted to the arts. The taxpayer has no direct control over how much he pays, or how the money is spent.

This is not the case with payments to the community out of the rent of land. This money corresponds in a precise way to the perceived value of the services actually received by the occupant of a site. The payment, then, is not a tax. It is a charge, global in character, but freely fixed by the occupier of land as the measure of the benefits that he actually expects to receive.

We know that the services that the prospective occupant wants are actually received, because he negotiated the rent before occupying the site: that is what happens in the market, when people buy and sell land. If they do not wish to use the services that are available, they express their preferences by moving to localities where their needs are more precisely met. Many people who retire, for example, do not wish to continue to receive - or pay for - amenities in large urban areas. In Britain, they prefer to move to the West Country, where services are fewer but more exactly in line with their requirements. Here, land is cheaper to rent. Childless couples, on the other hand, choose to move to more expensive residential areas because this is where they will gain access to the schools and clinics that they will require when they start their families. Here, the rent of land is expensive.

If the implementation of public policy is to be improved, it is important to employ the correct economic concepts. Thus, when we talk about the need to reform public finance, we have to recognise that people hate paying taxes; but they have no problem with paying for the benefits they receive. That is why it is necessary to stress that the payment of rent, to the community, is not a tax; it is a public charge, levied to pay for the services that people choose to receive.

The literature on tax policy, unfortunately, is riddled with weakness of exposition. Again, we turn to Kay and King for an illustration.

Successive governments in postwar Britain - both Labour and Conservative - have attempted to extract economic rent from the occupiers of land. Kay and King present some of the theory in relation to the way planning permission bumps up the price of land from its value in agricultural use (£5,000) to the £1m or more it can command as residential or commercial land. They note that, according to the theory, such a "tax" cannot be passed on to others. They then declare that "there is a weakness in this argument".

The supposed "weakness" is illustrated by a discussion of the dynamics of the land market. The developer could still make a profit, even if a large part of the capital gain were taken by the government. But: a sensible landowner would choose to squat on his site, hoping that the capital gains tax would be reduced or removed sometime in the future. This is what happened in postwar Britain. The response of landowners created an artificial scarcity in the supply of land, which drove up the price of other sites.

> Contrary to the expectations suggested by the theory of economic rent, a tax on gains from development levied in these circumstances would raise land prices, increase the scarcity of housing and housing land, and inhibit property development generally.[26]

In fact, this outcome does not in any way contradict the theory of economic rent. What it exposes is a flaw in the design of tax policy.

The public need to charge rent, payable whether one puts one's site to good use or not, is a lesson that has not yet been learnt by politicians. They can be excused; it is more difficult to understand why economic theorists continue to confound bad practise with good theory.

To gauge the practical effect of the modern reformulation of the theory of economic rent, we need only ask ourselves what possible purpose would be served by knowing that 95% of Pavarotti's income is really not wages at all, but economic rent. How does it help - from the points of view of public finance, or for the efficient allocation of resources between competing uses - to know that if Pavarotti were not an opera singer he would be singing for his supper in a barber's shop in Seville?

Kay and King, in referring to the rental value of the radio spectrum that was profitably exploited by broadcasters in the early years of commercial television in Britain, state that "the disadvantages of a high rate of tax on rents is that most of the costs of production are borne, in effect, by the taxpayer rather than by the company".[27] A high rate of "tax" on the annual rental value of a natural resource does not result in costs of production being borne by taxpayers. Anomalies that arise are the result of a flaw in the way the fiscal policy is designed; they are not the fault of the theory of rent, which is implied by the language used by the economists.

The guide to good policy is simple to conceive and execute: charge no more, and no less, than the annual rent of land and natural resources. Everything else falls into place, according to theory and long historical practise. Unfortunately, alas, we are not allowed to have it that easy. Economists have intervened in the democratic process to restrict debate to what they think is politically feasible. They have accomplished this astonishing feat by bending the meaning of the words we use, to the point where the rational conclusion - Rent = Public Revenue - is ridiculed as spurious.

Not all economists are guilty of confounding debate. A few of them have reached the correct conclusions, one of which reads like this:

> Thus, if the level of public expenditure is fixed, but the population is variable, the population that maximizes consumption per capita is such that rents equal public goods expenditure. This has been dubbed the "Henry George" theorem, since not only is the land tax non-distortionary, but also it is the "single tax" required to finance the public good.[28]

The man who dubbed the theorem "Henry George" is Joseph Stiglitz, now the professor of economics at Stanford University who was appointed by Bill Clinton to the President's Council of Economic Advisers.

Despite the obfuscation, eventually, somewhere, through weight of circumstance, a government will have to develop a clean slate strategy for public finance. Reform ought to occur sooner, rather than later, but the timing will depend largely on the ability of the electorate to apply democratic pressure. Without that pressure, politicians are likely to remain complacently cocooned in the failures of the past. They, after all, control the coercive means to cover up the problems of society, by squeezing the taxpayer for a little more money.

References

1. Tom Dale and Vernon Gill Carter, *Topsoil and Civilisation*, University ofOklahoma Press, 1955, cited in E.F. Schumacher, *Small is Beautiful*, London: Abacus, 1974, p.85.
2. C. Lowell Harriss, "Reducing Tax Obstacles to Economic Progress", Congress of Political Economists, Sydney, January 1994, mimeo., p.5.
3. Wallace Oates and Robert Schwab, *The Impact of Urban Land Taxation: The Pittsburgh Experience*, Cambridge, Mass.: Lincoln Institute of Land Policy, 1993. For a critique of this monograph, see Walt Rybeck, "Spectacular Pittsburgh findings emerge from land tax study", *Land and Liberty*, Jan. 1994, p.24.
In 1994, the Pittsburgh property tax rates were 18.45% on the assessed value of land, and 3.2% on buildings. A uniform tax rate, to raise the required revenue, would have been 5.8% on both land and buildings.
4. The results are published in *Incentive Taxation*, Henry George Foundation of America, 2000 Century Plaza, Suite 238, Columbia, MD 21044, USA.
5. Joseph Schumpeter, in his monumental history of economic philosophy, noted that "we cannot afford to pass by the economist [Henry George] whose individual success with the public was greater than that of all the others on our list". *History of Economic Analysis*, London: Routledge, 1954; p.864. Page references are to the Routledge edition, 1986.
6. *Ibid.*, p.865.
7. *Ibid.*
8. Cited in *Land & Liberty*, London, March-April 1932, p.35.
9. J.A. Kay and M.A. King, *The British Tax System* (1978); fifth edn., 1990. Oxford/New York: Oxford University Press, p.179.
10. Ronald Banks (editor), *Costing the Earth*, London: Shepheard-Walwyn, 1989.
11. Ronald Banks and Kenneth Jupp (Editors), *Private Property and Public Finance*, London: Shepheard-Walwyn/CIT, 1995.
12. Mason Gaffney and Fred Harrison, *The Corruption of Economics*, London: Shepheard-Walwyn/CIT, 1994.
13. *Op. cit.*, pp.932-938.
14. Banks and Jupp, *op. cit.*

15. Two authorities note that they would only "provide a (very) brief summary" of the work on optimal taxation. They do so in six paragraphs in a book of 274 pages. Simon James and Christopher Nobes, *The Economics of Taxation*, New York: Prentice Hall, 1978; 4th edn., 1992, pp.62-63.
16. *Op. cit.*, p.179.
17. *Op. cit.*, p.937, n.40.
18. James and Nobes, *op cit.*, devote 27 pages to considerations of equity in tax policy - compared with the one page devoted to a review of how to construct an optimum system.
19. Alfred Marshall, *Principles of Economics*, 4th edn., 1898, Bk. VI, Ch. II, Para.13.
20. Marshall illustrates the point with the example of a farmer: "[I]f he decides to have another plough instead of getting more work out of his present stock of ploughs, that will not make a lasting scarcity of ploughs since more ploughs can be produced to meet the demand: while, if he takes more land, there will be less left for others; since the stock of land in an old country cannot be increased. And this will be found to make the earnings of land enter into the problems of value and progress on a different footing from the earnings of implements made by man". *Ibid.*, p.478, n.1
21. A.R. Prest, *The Taxation of Urban Land*, Manchester: Manchester University Press, 1981, p.123.
22. *Ibid.*, pp.24-25.
23. *Ibid.*, pp.124-125.
24. B. Bittker, "A Comprehensive Income Tax Base as a Goal of Income Tax Reform", *Harvard Law Review*, Vol.80, 1967, p. 947.
25. Richard A. Musgrave, *Public Finance in a Democratic Society, Vol.1: Social Goods, Taxation and Fiscal Policy*, Brighton: Wheatsheaf Books, 1986, p.230.
26. *Op. cit.*, p.181.
27. *Ibid.*, pp.185-6.
28. Anthony B. Atkinson and Joseph E. Stiglitz, *Lectures on Public Economics*, London: McGraw-Hill, 1980, pp.524-25.

Contents

A Land as a Distinctive Factor of Production

B Major Economic Consequences

C Land-driven Booms and Busts

Land as a Distinctive Factor of Production
Mason Gaffney

The classical economists treated land as distinct from capital: "land, labour and capital" were the three basic "factors of production". They were mutually exclusive. They were comprehensive, including all economic agents. Each was also "limitational," meaning at least some of each was needed for all economic activity (v. A-9, below).[1] They made a coherent system.

Neo-classical economists denied the distinction and undertook to purge land from economese. Many of them, following John B. Clark and Frank Knight, still deny the distinction as I explain in *The Corruption of Economics*, a companion volume in this series. Many treat the matter by seizing on and stressing all similarities of land and capital, while ignoring all differences. Some invent gray areas that seem to fuse land and capital, present them as typical, and quickly move on. Many more simply ignore land, which has the effect of accepting the Clark-Knight verdict in practice. Others uneasily finesse and blur the issue by writing "land" in quotes, or trivializing its value, or referring vaguely to "quasi-rents" to comprehend a broad spectrum of incomes both from land and other factors.

Whatever possessed the neo-classicals to leave such a mess? One needs to know something of their times and politics. J.B. Clark and E.R.A. Seligman of Columbia University were obsessed with deflecting proposals, strongly supported at the time and place they wrote, to focus taxation on land. Henry George, after all, was nearly elected Mayor of New York City in 1886 and 1897. Frank Knight, founder of The Chicago School, followed them closely. That explains why some of the points made herein may seem

39

obvious to readers who have been spared the formal conditioning imposed on graduate students in economics. In graduate training, however, the obvious is obscured, silenced, or denied. Hundreds of books on economic theory are published with "land" absent from the index. Denial is reinforced by dominant figures using sophistical, pedantic cant, which students learn to ape to distinguish themselves from the laity and advance their careers.[2]

The dominance of "fusers" is shown by the prevalence of 2-factor models, wherein the world is divided into just labour and capital.[3] Land is melded with capital, and simply disappears as a separate category, along with its distinctive attributes. A number of economists don't buy it, but don't do anything about it - acquiescing in error by silence, indifference, passivity, or anxiety of the professional consequences. They handle the question by "going into denial," as it were, resolving a vexing issue by pretending it isn't there. Truth will not be made manifest by hedging, especially against such motivated forces as have an interest in hiding unearned wealth behind the skirts of capital.

The market exchange of capital for land causes an elementary failure in the minds of many. Land and capital each have their prices and may be bought and sold for money. Each alike is part of an invidividual's assets, colloquially called his "capital". Each is a store of value to the individual. What is true of each individual must be true for all together, is the thinking: it is the "fallacy of composition." We will see herein that society cannot turn land into capital (A-6), and land is not a store of value for society (A-10).

The discipline has not totally eliminated land, but marginalized it. There is a subdiscipline called "Land Economics," and a journal of that name. There are journals of Agricultural Economics, Urban Economics, Regional Science, Environmental Economics, Natural Resources, and more. There are also whole disciplines of Geography, Economic Geography, Military Science, Biogeography, Geology, Geometry, Surveying, Astronomy, Theology, Ecology, Oceanography, Meteorology, Soils, Physiography, Topography, and Hydrology, all dealing with The Earth and Nature and Creation as definable topics distinct from man's works.

The subdisciplines are kept away from the "core" and "mainstream" of economic thinking by compartmentalization and colonialization. Patronizing "land economics" as a colonial discipline keeps potentially contagious movements within the empire, where they can absorb critical tendencies under watchful control, while yet remaining safely remote, in the outskirts of the system. Orthodoxy flows out from the core, communicated via mandatory "core courses." Land economics is banished from the "commanding heights" of money and banking, macro policy, and required "basic" courses in methodology and micro theory.

Colonial life is safe and easy, if dull and unfulfilling, but once labelled "colonial" one is supposed to remain in the assigned cage. One who attempts integration is "overambitious," and "spread too thin". Colonials are not supposed to relate land economics to unemployment, inflation, financial collapse, deficit finance, and such core topics. They become unwitting co-conspirators in marginalizing their subject.

Micro theory is the inmost citadel of holy writ, where "the economic way of thinking" is inculcated. It is required of all economics students before they venture into real issues. It becomes their shibboleth, their lingua franca, and shapes their worldview. Within common micro theory, to the extent it relates to real life at all, the technique has been first to relegate production economics to a minor role: "price theory" comes first. Production economics deals with the optimal combination of inputs in production, and how this relates to their relative costs. That should lead right into factoral distribution, but this aspect is soft-pedaled or omitted entirely. This omission alone is a fatal fault, considering that the forces determining land rents vary inversely with those determining rates of return on capital (cf. A-7 below).

Within production economics, "variable proportions" with "factor symmetry" replaces diminishing returns. The parcel of land disappears as a unit of analysis, replaced by "the firm," a disembodied spirit that combines resources optimally, treating all alike as variable "in the long run." In the "short run," land is subsumed in "fixed costs"; rising demand that raises rents is just "imputed away" silently and lumped with other elements of "fixed cost." If that sounds muddled, it is because what it describes is muddled.[4]

Common micro theory finesses Time. It deals with economic relations as though they occurred at a point in time. Sometimes two points are allowed (short run and long). Thus micro theory can ignore the birth of capital, its growth, maturity, senescence, death, burial, and replacement, vital elements of its difference from land. Time, and relations of sequence, are hived off to the far satellite of "finance," usually not even taught in departments of economics. Time is also referred to under "history of economic thought," as an obsession of some 19th century Austrians who wrote quaintly of "roundabout" (time-using) methods of production.[5] Relations of sequence are found in macro, but not firmly integrated with micro theory, which is the enduring core of the discipline. Micro theory still deals with relations of coexistence in time, and space as well. As A.A. Milne once wrote, "It isn't really anywhere, it's somewhere else instead." Of neo-classical theory we may add, "It isn't really anytime, it's some other time instead."[6]

All that is confusing for students and others. Land does have distinctive qualities for economic analysis and policy. This essay gives 10 primary reasons why land is distinct from capital (and of course from mankind itself) as an economic input. Then it gives 18 important economic consequences thereof, and their policy implications. Making land markets, land policy, and land taxation work well for the general welfare is a major challenge for economists and statesmen. They have neglected it too long by crediting and following the peculiar neo-classical sophisms that obscure or deny all distinctions between land and capital.

A

Primary Distinctions

A-1. Land is not produced nor reproduceable

Land is not produced, it was created. It is the world, the planet from which man evolved, with the sun that energizes it and the orbit that tempers it. Land is a free gift, variously expressed in different philosophies as Spaceship Earth, the Big Blue Marble, God's Gift, Creation, Gaia, The Promised Land, or Nature. Mankind did not create The Earth with its space and resources, nor can we add to them. We can only acquire them, often by fighting, or rent-seeking, or in other counterproductive ways. Man at best improves and develops capacities inherent in the free gift. It is disappointing, and should alert us and make us suspicious, that economic analysis would ever purge out this paramount, self-evident truth.

"Land" in economics means all natural resources and agents, with their sites (locations and extensions in space). Land is not just the matter occupying space: it *is* space. It includes many things not colloquially called land, such as water and the beds under it, the radio spectrum, docks, rights of way, take-off/landing time slots for aircraft, aquifers, ambient air (the right to breathe it and the license to pollute), "air rights" to strata in the third dimension of cities, falling water, wild fish, game, and vegetation, natural scenery, weather, the environment, the ecology, the natural gene pool, etc. Any franchise, license or privilege giving territorial rights is a species of easement over land. Your driver's license is a right to use land: red lights remind us of the critical value of space at central locations, since two objects cannot occupy the same space at the same time. It is worth a lot to have the right-of-way, as railroads do.

Economic land excludes many things, too, that are colloquially called

43

land. It excludes land-fill, for example, by which many cities are extended into shallow waters. The site and seabed are properly land; the land-fill is an improvement. There is no "made land" in the economic sense: it is reallocated from other uses. Expanding cities take farmland from producing food and fiber, much of it for the expanding city itself. Filled land in shallow water near cities is taken away from anglers and sailors and viewers and ecologists, who now routinely organize to save it from being "made" away with. Drained and filled wetlands are taken away from endangered species, as well as from their primal role as filters protecting coastal waters from river trash and pollutants. Thanks to the myopia and dereliction of economists, it has taken militant environmentalists to carry home this truth, developing in their struggle to be heard and understood a deep skepticism of economists and their "way of thinking."

Capital is that which has been produced but not yet used up. Capital is formed by human thrift, forebearance, investment and production. Only after mankind forms and makes capital does it bear much likeness to land, in that they coexist. Ordinary micro-economics obscures the differences because it deals mainly with relations of coexistence, ignoring the continual formation and destruction of capital, ignoring time and relations of sequence. Thus it excludes from its purview one of the prime differences between land and capital. The life of capital, like that of people, is marked by major sacraments of birth, growth, aging and death - all missing from micro theory. Micro deals mainly with how existing resources are allocated at a moment in time, not how they originate, grow, flourish, reproduce, age, die, and decompose.

Capital occupies space; land *is* space. In common micro theory, resources and markets come together at a point not just in time but in space. Again, it excludes from its purview one of the prime qualities of land.

For the reasons given, alone, land and capital are mutually exclusive.

A-2. Land as site is permanent and recyclable
Land as "site" (location plus extension) does not normally wear out, depreciate, spoil, obsolesce, nor get used up by human activities incident to occupancy and production. In contrast, capital depreciates from time and use, routinely and by nature. After being formed, it must be conserved from entropy by continual maintenance, repair, remodeling, safeguarding against

theft and fire, and so on. Like our own bodies, it returns to dust; land is the dust to which it returns. Inventories are depleted; moving parts wear out; fixed capital depreciates with use and time.[7]

Land normally does not depreciate as a function of time. Most attributes of land also withstand use and abuse. Most land is, rather, expected to appreciate in real value in the long run. Values go in cycles, but the secular history is upwards as population, capital, and demands all grow while land remains fixed. Capital has a period of formation during which it accretes value by storing up other inputs and changing physical form, but that is a phase. Once formed, almost all capital fails with time.

Perhaps the most durable capital is intellectual, like the writings of Plato. These, however, do not endure generations without the continual human effort and expense of education. As schools starve and libraries close, it is sadly certain that much will be lost. Under any conditions much is twisted in transmission, like classical economics itself.

Capital, however durable, also obsolesces because it is subject to continual competition from streams of new products. Intellectual capital, however classic, is subject to endless competition from floods of new ideas and discoveries. Land does not obsolesce from this cause: there is no new land, let alone modern, state-of-the-art land. Both land and capital are subject to demand-obsolescence from changes in tastes and fashions, but overall the taste for land as a consumer good rises as incomes and wealth grow. The writer has documented elsewhere how the land share of residential real estate value rises sharply with its total value.[8] The land part of residential real estate is a "superior good"; the building part is not.

It follows that the demand for land rises over time with incomes, but faster than incomes. For example, the soaring demand for golf has produced 150 golf courses in one California county (Riverside) alone, preempting a good bit of the usable land and a huge share of this natural desert's limited water resources. The western quarter of Massachusetts, the Berkshires, with adjoining parts of Connecticut, New York, and Vermont, has become one vast country estate for suburban New Yorkers and pensioners, and is priced high above its farm value. Ski resorts, hunting clubs, yacht harbours, spas, beach resorts, and such uses increasingly outbid mere utilitarian uses for prime lands. There is also a high and rising technical multiplier of demand for land to complement modern consumer capital. For example, the parking demands alone of 200 million private cars in the USA. preempt an area as large as Maryland and Delaware combined. Soaring demands and reuse values are thus the norm in an affluent society.

What can it mean to "consume" land, when it does not get used up? It can only mean to occupy or preempt a time-slot of space. That has the most profound implications for the meaning of "consumption" in economic thinking, and "consumer taxation" in fiscal policy. Economists have neglected and papered over these matters almost completely. These are pursued in B-13 below.

Some attributes of some lands do deteriorate from some uses or abuses. Extractive resources call for special analysis, which the writer has attempted elsewhere.[9] To avoid lengthy repetition from previous publications, the word "land" herein refers to the permanent qualities of land, exemplified by (but not limited to) site. Remember, land is not just matter, it is space itself.[10] It is not unusual for land first to be mined, then used for dumping wastes, then sealed over for urban use. I myself have lived comfortably over an old munitions dump on Lockehaven Drive, Victoria, B.C.

Land is reusable. All the land we have is second-hand, most of it previously-owned. Our descendants, in turn, will have nothing but our hand-me-downs. As there is never any new supply, the old is recycled periodically, and will be in perpetuity, without changing form or location. Melded briefly with fixed buildings, land survives them to go one more round of use. Even while melded with capital, land is fit for another use at any time, unlike the capital on it. Land retains a practicable, measurable, meaningful opportunity cost. Land value in cities may be defined as "what is left after a good fire"; arsonists take that quite literally. In Beverly Hills, California, "tear-downs" are routine as taste-obsolescence races through fashionable neighbourhoods where the land outvalues even the elegant buildings. These are dated after thirty years.

The opportunity cost of capital is fleeting. Capital loses most of it the moment it is committed to a specific form, whose physical alternative use is often only as scrap. Land's "opportunity cost" is real and viable at all times. The scrap value of capital is often zero or negative (radioactive waste supplying an extreme example).

Land may be afflicted with such "negative capital," the harmful waste from prior usage. An example is the spent carcass of an old building needing costly demolition. Some would class that spent carcass as a subtraction from the site value, but "negative capital" makes more sense, as may be inferred by considering the relations between a landlord and a tenant in a perfect market. The lease holds the tenant liable for damages he does and wastes he leaves; the prudent landlord requires of the tenant a deposit, or in larger cases a bond, to assure performance. Both acknowledge that damage done by use is imputed to the user, not to the land.[11]

Too often, from institutional or market or human failure, the land is left damaged, with no recourse against those responsible. Then, indeed, the damage becomes part of the land, just as some of the good relics of history may as well be considered part of the land. Toxic wastes, and endemic parasites imported with previous crops or trees, become mixed into the dirt. We do not trivialize nor quibble over what to call such damage: it happens, and it impairs the reuse value of land. In such cases the site is less valuable, but still permanent and recyclable. Such cases are, fortunately, still more the exception than the rule. They are at most a minor qualification to the major points made here.

Physical abuse of land is less a problem, actually, than the fall of value that results from social decay. Much of land value is a social product. When a society sickens, declines, and self-destructs, as we know may happen, it lowers ground rents, which mirror social progress and decay. We cannot surely forecast that our own society will not self-destruct, as parts of cities already have. However, until it does, land will outlast capital economically. Even when it does, landownership may remain the last bastion, as happened in the feudal system. Even if barbarians overrun us, it is the land they will take: little else will remain.

A-3. Land supply is fixed
Being both unreproducible and permanent, land remains fixed.[12] Both the overall quantity and the special qualities of specific lands remain fixed. Capital changes its form and location with each turnover, while land remains the same. The Tyler Galleria neighbourhood in Riverside, California, makes an example. In the last fifteen years over half the buildings have been replaced or heavily remodeled. Streets have been repaved and widened; utilities enhanced. Inventories have turned over hundreds of times; cars in the parking lots have come and gone thousands of times. The land is the

same.

The fixity of land has several aspects.

a. The overall planet is fixed.

Even the planet may change, but "fixed" here means "given" or "exogenous" or "outside individual control," not necessarily static. Cosmic and tectonic and climatic changes are given, so far as man is concerned. Changes caused by mankind collectively are given so far as individual landowners are concerned.

b. Land is fixed within political jurisdictions.

Political jurisdictions are defined as areas of land. Capital and labour cross political boundary lines; land stays put. An "open economy" is open to money and goods, to capital and labour, not to land. For tax consequences, cf. A-4 and B-5 below.

c. Land as site is immobile in space, permanently.[13]

Much capital, on the other hand, is physically mobile by wheel, hoof, wing or boat. California calls this "unsecured" property, and France calls it *"meubles"*, as distinct from the other kind which is "secured" and *"immeuble."*[14] Most American jurisdictions use the less expressive "personal" and "real" property for the same distinction.

Secured or "real" capital is capital affixed to land. The physical carcass of most buildings is rooted to the spot, leading some to allege buildings are as fixed in location as land. That would be specious, economically. The capital locked up in the carcasses of buildings is normally recovered, as they depreciate, in Capital Consumption Allowances (CCAs) which may be reinvested anywhere.

"Basic" micro economic theory, as ordinarily ordained today, is constructed so as to paper over this basic difference of land and capital. In its "short run" land and capital are both fixed. In its "long run" both are equally variable to "the firm," the disembodied spirit used as its unit of analysis, existing at a point in time and space. Thus, one can specialize for a lifetime in "basic micro" while remaining unaware that capital, over time, changes its form and location as it turns over, unlike land. Land yields no such mobile funds as CCAs. It does not depreciate, and is priced accordingly higher, so its income is only enough to yield a return on the price paid, not a return of it. This is refuted below.

Land is "mobile" only in the limited sense that its use may change. Some micro economists would have this sort of "mobility" equate land to capital. See A-5,a, below.

d. Land is fixed in form.

Capital, in contrast, is Protean, assuming one form after another. Capital is also fungible with each turnover. Capital Consumption Allowances in money join the common worldwide pool of disposable capital. Money itself is not capital, but is generalized command over a share of the flow of current production. Thus, capital loses its specific identity with each turnover.

e. Acquiring land must mean taking others'.

No one can get more land without others keeping less. One can acquire more capital by forming it through saving and investing. One can consume more by working more, while others work no less. Land is different: it is the most common basis of market power, therefore (cf. B-11, below).

A-4. Land is immobile in space and uncontrollable in time

a. Land does not migrate.

When demand grows for land in a specific area or neighbourhood, land cannot immigrate to meet the higher demand. It is true that land elsewhere can be converted to the specific land use that is demanded. Some micro theorists argue that this makes land as "mobile" as anything else, which equates land and capital. It dovetails with and reinforces their paradigm centred on "the firm," a unit that can add unlimited inputs of all kinds in the long run, and among which competition drives all profits to zero. This rationalization overlooks the hoary adage of real estate: "value depends on three factors, location, location, and location." What happens then is not that supply rises to meet higher demand, but ground rent rises.

Robert Triffin wrote that "excess returns are either competed away, or imputed away." Excess returns to capital are the ones that get competed away; excess returns to land get imputed away. Rents and land prices rise where demand is focused. Interest rates, the cost of capital, do not rise: capital abhors a vacuum, and rushes in to bring returns back down to the common worldwide level. If anything, interest rates are lower in central cities because of the more perfect markets that develop there. Intensive development and use of the third dimension at the hub of a city makes it even more attractive, through synergy (conglomerate increasing returns to scale), raising rents still more.

b. The services of land flow and perish with time.

Land is "immobile in time" in the sense that its services flow steadily with time. They cannot be stored and shifted forward to meet anticipated higher future demand, like stored goods. They cannot be bunched, like military tanks for an attack. One cannot reach into the future and marshal them for present needs or emergencies. They are never "on tap," for drawing down at will; neither may they be set aside for future use. Rather they flow down the river and out the gates of time to sink forever into the dead past.

Land services may be and are used to produce capital, and the capital is stored up. An example is land used for growing timber, or raising seedlings to bearing age. Another example is flowing water stored in a reservoir. This does not convert land into capital, however, any more than it converts labour into capital. Stored-up labour and land-service *are* capital: that is what capital is, by definition.[15] Nature's services *per se*, however, come in a flow like time itself, unbidden and uncontrollable. Mankind cannot advance nor retard its services at will. Considering the improvident nature of mankind that is perhaps a good thing, but good or bad, it is so.[16]

Land titles serve as "stores of value" for individual owners. By the common fallacy of composition, plus some confusion, that makes it all too easy for laymen, and economists too, to think of land as a store of social value. The individual can tap this store, however, only by selling it to another. Neither of them can advance or retard the flow of services at will.

Usually the given flow is steady or seasonal, but not always or necessarily. Seasons change, climates change, environments change, blights and pestilences come and go. The essence of land service flow is not steadiness, but exogeneity. Alfred Marshall defined the "public value of land" as the product of three factors exogenous to the private owner: nature, public services, and spillovers from the use of nearby private land. This "neo-classical" was classically right on this point (great economists seldom fit snugly into tight boxes).

c. Land is not uniform to a user or firm.

When a firm adds land to its operation, the added land is normally farther from the firm's nucleus and not, therefore, homogeneous. The added land is marginal to the firm in location, not just in quantity. The marginal location means that more internal transportation cost is required to integrate the added land with the operation. That is a prime diseconomy of scale, limiting the optimal area of producing units.

As a firm expands it takes land from the margins of neighbouring firms. As Firm A continues to expand, the zone of acquisition moves farther from A's nucleus, but closer to that of B, its neighbour. As the zone advances, the contested land becomes of higher value to B, and lower value to A. Again, this is a matter both of pure quantity and specific location. Military Science would produce few winners if it aped Economics and ignored such facts.

It is different when a growing firm adds labour and capital to its operation. These are drawn from the margins of other operations, but they are marginal only in quantity, not location. They are homogenous units, and may be added to the core of the growing operation. That continues to be so, however much Firm A grows, or B shrinks. This is because labour and capital migrate, and their supplies are a "pool." No one neighbour is singled out for raiding; there is no locational factor.

This locational factor qualifies the idea of "factor symmetry," as developed by Clark and Wicksteed,[16a] and expressed in the replacement of "diminishing returns" by "variable proportions" in economic analysis. It is impossible to add "homogeneous" land to an operation: each unit has a unique location, and added land is normally farther from the nucleus.

This consideration, taken alone, would make landholdings tend toward uniformity, to minimize internal transport costs. In fact, however, landholdings are less uniform than other measures of firm size, like labour force, capital improvements, sales, and value-added. These facts are consistent with an hypothesis that the acquisition of land as a store of value, dominated by financial forces tending toward concentration, interferes with efficiency in land markets. This hypothesis is further considered in B-11.

Added land, besides being farther from a nucleus, may be farther from a street interface. In retailing this is extremely weighty. Land added to water front parcels may be far from the shore, and so on.

d. Land division is a highly social process.

i) Land division entails "packing."

One individual parcel does not expand or contract without impacting the whole system. Parcels have common boundaries and must be packed together so that they all fit. Many costs like fencing and roads and utilities are shared along the common boundaries. These costs vary with the length of the boundaries.

ii) Capital and labour come in "nuclei."

Each parcel has its nucleus, as, for example, a farm centres on its farmstead.[17] The nucleus is the indivisible core of labour/capital applied to the land. Land division entails more nuclei, hence greater intensity of land use, for whatever purpose.

"Nucleus" here is a proxy for labour/capital, although one nucleus is not a fixed quantity of labour/capital. Generally the nucleus shrinks as the acreage shrinks, but in lesser proportion, so intensity of land use rises.

e. Nuclei are interdependent.

In finding the optimal resultant of these opposing forces we are faced with more than a standard example of diminishing returns. One could perceive land division as simply a matter of applying more people and capital to a given area of land. The more intensive application to each acre justifies itself up to a point by added yields from each acre; beyond that the added yields do not compensate for the added costs.

But there is more here than a simple matter of quantities and proportions of inputs. There is also a distance factor. The more parcels we add the closer are their nuclei, and the less is the cost of linking them along the common lines. The cost per acre is, to be sure, higher: that is inherent in adding more labour and capital to a given amount of land. But the linkage cost per parcel drops as we add nuclei by dividing land into more parcels.

There is an asymmetry here that has been obscured in the evolution of marginal productivity theory, with its effort to show that the relationships among all the classical factors of production are "symmetrical," so that diminishing returns is simply variable proportions. Land is not symmetrical with labour/capital. When you add nuclei of labour/capital to land, they get packed closer together. But when you add land to fixed labour and capital, the units all get farther apart — the land units as well as the nuclei of labour/ capital.

f. Land is immobile among taxing jurisdictions.

Tax jurisdictions are specific areas of land: they are defined that way. Land cannot escape from taxation, therefore (cf. A-3). Further, it follows that all purely local taxes are shifted to land, whatever the nominal base of the tax (cf. B-5). If the application of labour and capital to land yields no surplus or rent, there is no tax base: any attempt to tax the labour and capital must simply drive them away, unless the use of the taxes itself creates rent. This is the "Physiocratic law of tax incidence".[18] Likewise, purely local services add to land rents.

A-5. Land does not turn over. It is recycled and is versatile
a. Land is not convertible into other land.

Each unit of land is permanently unique. Capital, on the other hand, is a homogeneous "pool" over time: as each unit degrades and yields back its substance, the owner may reinvest the Capital Consumption Allowances in anything. Thus, capital is fungible: one specific item of capital is universally convertible into any other. Land is not at all fungible: no specific unit of land is convertible into any other.

J.B. Clark tried to wipe out this distinction, which brought him into debate with Boehm-Bawerk over whether capital has a "period of production". Frank Knight, following Clark, renewed the debate with Friedrich von Hayek. The intent of both Clark and Knight was to shelter land behind the skirts of capital, to counter a popular movement for taxing land more and capital less. Students are still required to study these dreary, mystical exchanges, which seem to have no other purpose.

The rate of turnover of capital may vary, and does, over a wide range, from once a day for restaurant fresh vegetables to once a century for slow-growth timber. Thus, the "valency" with which capital combines with labour is highly variable. The land/labour valency is not fixed, but it contains no such extreme factor as this.

b. Land is necessarily versatile.

Capital is made to order for specific needs. Land must serve all of man's needs of the day, and perpetual streams, waves, and eddies of new fads and demands, with no physical change.

New demands and discoveries bring out new virtues in old land but it is man that has changed, not land. The resources were always there waiting.

In the long run, the pool of capital is totally versatile as old specialized capital wears out and is replaced with new. Thus, land is less versatile than capital regarded as a pool in the long run. However, existing specialized capital, committed to a specific form, loses most of its opportunity cost. Capital suffers from various kinds of obsolescence, including, when affixed to land, locational obsolescence. Land rarely does. Land's opportunity cost remains a viable option, because the only source of land for new uses today, as for ages past, is to take it from its previous use. Even land taken from the Indians, as they keep reminding us, had a previous use.

It is the common markets in labour, capital and commodities that exert the common influences. The versatility of individual land parcels is often considerable, it is true. Land in the long run is more versatile than is specialized existing capital in the short run. Comparing long run with long run, however, it is capital that is totally versatile.

  c. Land *per se* is economically divisible, unlike capital.

Since land does not have to be produced, it can be divided into parcels as small as you please. Capital is economically indivisible, an economist's word which does not mean quite what it appears to. One can produce very small trucks or ships or buildings, but the cost per unit of useful capacity rises as they get smaller: that is "indivisibility." Its converse is economy of scale.

Economies of scale are inherent attributes of capital and labour, not land. They spring from using large units of capital; or large teams of workers with specialized members. For this large lands are required, but the scale economies are not in the land. It is usually a social diseconomy to acquire large lands because they impinge on others and push them out of the way. Thus a large truck requires more street space which may require widening streets which take land from the buildings between the streets. Large buildings require either land assembly, or prior withholding of land over long periods, or going to bad locations on cheap land. All of these are costly.

In subdividing land into small parcels there are, it is true, extra costs, but the cost per lot falls. Of course the cost per square foot rises, but the cost per dollar of value created generally also falls, which is why it is done. Apartments, condominia, strata titles and time-sharing represent extreme subdivision without increasing cost.

Those who require much land normally have limited choice of locations: they must go where land may be had in large pieces. It is either that, or buy it already assembled by others, that is not so true of those who need large labour or capital inputs.

  d. It is cheaper to build units of capital all at once.

Capital, unlike land, has to be built. Normally capital will retain through life its original scale, and other basic characteristics, because it is so costly to add-on after construction. Buildings are adapted to particular sites when built, and are seldom raised or lowered after construction. (Capital in its making has economies both of scale, and "simultaneity".)

A-6. Land is not interchangeable with capital

Land is not convertible into capital, nor *vice versa*. Exchange of land for capital has misled many into equating them, but only through inadvertence and the fallacy of composition. Exchange is not interchange: exchange does not change the quantity of either land or capital. Capital is convertible into any other form of capital each time it turns over, by using Capital Consumption Allowances, the proceeds of turnover, to hire people actually to produce new capital. Capital may also be disinvested and consumed, or augmented by new saving and investment. None of those is true of land.

The fact above seems simple when laid out overtly, yet economists overlook it when they frame tax policy. Nonconvertibility gives an entirely new meaning to the old goal of "uniformity" in taxation, belying the notion that uniformity makes for a "level playing field", or neutrality in taxation. Uniformity is desirable to avoid "excise tax" effects, but that end does not require uniformity as between land and capital, only uniformity within each class. Cf. B-6.

A-7. Land rents are subject to market forces that differ from those that determine interest rates (the price of capital)

Interest rates around the world rise and fall in sympathy. They are subject to common, interconnecting forces of supply and demand, transmitted swiftly even in past centuries, and today instantaneously.

Land rents, too, rise and fall together in response to common forces. However, the forces are different for land rents than for interest rates, so they do not vary in sympathy. Even though the lands are not mutually convertible, they are subject to common forces, the greatest of which is the interest rate itself. Capital and land are rivals for the same pie, so usually their returns vary inversely. Ground rent equals operating cash flow less interest on the cost of building, and less building depreciation. A rise of interest rates lowers ground rents.

It is hard to see how any forecast of the results of economic policy, or any forecast for investment purposes, could have any value without keeping focused on this distinction. Sometimes it is handled by distinguishing "old" from "new" assets or issues. Yet, in general, neo-classical doctrine tells us to meld land and capital in economic thinking of all kinds.

A-8. Land price guides investors and determines the character of capital, as capital substitutes for land

High land price guides investors to prefer kinds of capital that substitute for land. Although capital cannot be converted into land, it can substitute for land, and does so when rents and land prices are high. John Stuart Mill long ago pointed out that the structure and character of capital is determined by the level of rents and wages.[19] Such substitution is an integral part of the equilibrating function of markets; the human race could never have attained its present numbers and density without it. High wages evoke labour-saving capital; high rents evoke land-saving capital. It is useful to carry this farther, and recognize five kinds of substitutive capital evoked by high rents and land prices:

    a. Land-saving capital, like high buildings.

    b. Land-enhancing capital, meaning capital used to improve land for a new, higher use.

    c. Land-linking capital, like canals and rails and city streets.

    d. Land-capturing (rent-seeking) capital, like squatters' improvements, and canal and rail lines built to secure land grants, and dams and canals built to secure water rights.

    e. Rent-leading capital.

These are defined and discussed in Section C-3.

    To understand the forces shaping capital investment, one must recognize the difference of land and capital. High land prices evoke substitution of capital for land, shaping the capital stock in particular ways. Viewed positively, this is a central part of economic equilibration, tempering land scarcity. Viewed negatively, it has led historically to boom and bust cycles (cf. C-3).

A-9. Land is limitational

Land and capital are mutually exclusive. Each is also limitational, meaning all human activity requires at least some of each.

Land is indispensable to life, hence to economic activity. The same is generally true of labour and capital, but less "absolutely". Land can exist perfectly well without labour or capital, and support timber and wildlife, but labour and capital cannot exist at all without at least some land, and often a great deal of land. Substitution is limited. It will not do just to have 57 varieties of labour, or of capital. There must be at least some land. Remember, land includes space itself, and a time-slot in it. It includes air and water, the environment and the ecology and all original matter itself. Without land there is nothing.[20] Coupling this with the non-reproduceability of land, and its fixity, land is distinctive.

"Homelessness," a modern plague, is essentially landlessness. A popular ditty from the 1930s includes the catchy line, "If you can't pay the rent, you can live in a tent," but you can't do even that without a campsite. Perhaps this is why modern economists have so little to say about homelessness. Joblessness they have dismissed as part of the vital economic function of "job-seeking," with which they have persuaded at least themselves. The next logical step is that the person sleeping in the doorway is not really homeless, but just engaged in the vital market function of "home-seeking". Rather than seem totally absurd they are simply silent, except to stress the "exclusionary principle" of private property as the bedrock of their system, and their system as a panacea.

In this they are out of step with general thinking. In France, at least, polls have shown for several years the two most respected and popular figures are the Abbé Pierre, who crusades for the homeless, and Jacques Cousteau the environmentalist, who also preaches on the folly of ignoring the limitational nature of land.

There is scope for massive substitution of land for labour and capital, and labour and capital for land. That is, the proportions in which we combine the factors are variable. This substitution cannot, however, be carried so far as to dispense with land altogether: this is the meaning of limitational.[21] Piling more capital on the same land is limited by diminishing returns.

Therefore the three factors are always found working in combination, and much of economic theory used to deal with how they are combined. Some of it still does; the rest floats in outer space, perhaps communing with the ghost of Plato.

A-10. Land value is not an economic fund
Economists teach that all economic values are either funds or flows. It is
a seductive division, and often useful, but too simple by far. Land value is
neither, but a third kind of value, *sui generis*. Mankind cannot add to it, nor
draw from it as from a true fund. Individuals can and do, by exchange. Even
nations can, by selling to aliens. Thanks to the fallacy of composition that
lets us forget that these are merely intermediate transactions which
collectively accomplish nothing. In famine, or war, or capital shortage,
society cannot live on land values. These are not accumulations of stores,
but merely the present value of anticipated future service flows which
cannot be hastened.

Further divisions are distinctive too, in other contexts. Exhaustible
resources (excluded from this discussion) could be called "natural funds."
Fixed capital, slowly depreciating with time, is a "flowing fund." Soils have
additional components. But basic permanent location value, our present
focus, is in no way an economic "fund."

SUMMARY

Land and capital[22] are mutually exclusive categories, provided that
"exclusive" is understood properly.

a. Some of each is essential to production.

b. They are not mutually convertible.

They are substitutable (see above), but convertible is different. Capital
and labour in the long run (not very long, for most capital) are fungible
pools as they reproduce and replace themselves, generation following
generation. That is, all capital is convertible into any other form of capital
when it is replaced. It is not convertible into land. That is one implication
of "mutually exclusive."

Capital is fungible in the long run, i.e. every unit or "molecule" is
convertible to any other. Labour is slightly less so, and the generations are
longer.[23]

Thus, all capital tends to earn the same rate of return at the margin. There
is a "pool" of capital, whose returns are subject to common influences. The
labour pool is more differentiated, but still, all wage and salary rates are
subject to common influences through the interflow caused by competition

and mobility. In the long run, replaceability of capital makes individual "capitals" totally fungible, i.e. perfect substitutes for each other — but not for land. So it is, too, with labour, without the same perfection.

Land rents tend to rise and fall together, too, being subject to common influences: direct demand, indirect demand via commodity prices, input costs, wage rates, and real interest rates.

B

Major Economic Consequences

B-1. The origin of property in land is not economic
    a. Politics guides the original distribution.
    The initial distribution of land - the origin of property in land - is military, legal, and political, not economic. The prime business of nations throughout history has been to gain and defend land. What was won by force has no higher sanction than *lex fortioris*, and must be kept and defended by force.

    After land is appropriated by a nation the original distribution is political. The nature of societies, cultures and economies for centuries afterwards are molded by that initial distribution, exemplified by the differences between Costa Rica (equal partition) and El Salvador with its fabled "Fourteen Families" (*Las Catorce*), or between Canada and Argentina.

    Political redistribution also occurs within nations, as with the English enclosures and Scottish "clearances," when one part of the population in effect conquered the rest by political machinations, and took over their land, their source of livelihood. Reappropriation and new appropriation of tenures is not just an ancient or a sometime thing but an ongoing process. This very day proprietary claims to water sources, pollution rights, access to rights of way, radio spectrum, signal relay sites, landing rights, beach access, oil and gas, space on telephone and power poles (e.g. for cable TV), taxi licences, etc. are being created under our noses. In developing countries of unstable government the current strong man often grants concessions to imperialistic adventurers who can bolster his hold on power by supplying both cash up front, and help from various US and UN agencies from the IMF to the United States Marine Corps.

60

Ordinary economic thinking today would have it that a nation that distributes land among private parties by "selling to the highest bidder" is using an economic method of distribution. Such thinking guides World Bank and IMF economists as they advise nations emerging from communism on how to privatize land. The neutrality is specious, at best. Even selling to the high bidder is a political decision, as 19th century American history makes clear.

i) The right to sell was won by force, is not universally honoured, and must be kept by continuous use of force.

ii) In practice, selling for cash up front reserves most land for a few with front-money advantage, inside information, good contacts, corrupt aids, etc. The history of disposal of US public domain leaves no doubt about this and it is still going on with air rights, water, radio, landing rights, fishing licenses, etc. Choices being made currently are just as tainted as those of 19th century history.

Selling land in large blocks under frontier conditions is to sell at a time before it begins yielding much if any rent. It is bid in by those few who have large discretionary funds of patient money. Politicians, meantime, treat the proceeds as current revenues used to hold down other taxes today, leaving the nation with inadequate revenues in the future.

iii) The ability to bid high does not necessarily come from legitimate saving. The early wealth of Liverpool came from the slave trade. High bidders for many properties today are middle eastern potentates who neither produced nor saved the wealth they control. Other high bidders are criminals, who find the "sanctity of property" a splendid route for laundering their gains, and a permanent shelter against further prosecution.

Apart from such obvious cases, more generally, control over front money, however honestly acquired historically, is a factor separate from the ability to use land productively. This is addressed below, in B-8.

This matter of the origins of property in land is skirted, ignored, obscured, or trivialized by libertarian (neo-anarchist) philosophers, e.g. the Chicago School, and their lead is followed by the mass of economists today.[24] It is the Achilles' heel of these and allied philosophies. One of these, the contract theory of the state, was heavily used to sell Proposition 13 in California in 1978. Howard Jarvis, the author and protagonist, repeated daily that "Property should pay only for services to property, not services to people." "Services to property" he construed very narrowly indeed.

Ownership and tenure rights derive only from appropriation, not saving, investment or production. Capital, by contrast, is owned by those who formed it.

     c. Inertia takes over after the original distribution, perpetuating and aggravating it.

Inertia, both financial and political, transmitted through generations by inheritance, is a major control over the distribution of wealth and income. How else can one explain their exceedingly distorted distributions, in contrast with the normal distribution of most human abilities? Inertia extends the original pattern for generations. More, the advantages given by controlling discretionary funds (those not needed for subsistence) magnify the original political result.

"Positive" economists and Libertarians, who fancy they have found in private property rights a "value-free," apolitical basis for thinking about and structuring society, have to paper over the political origins of landownership. If one's grandfather was a slave when the Land Office was parcelling out Federal lands to the friends and cousins of corrupt Congressmen, one may be excused from believing Utopia will ensue from limiting all future changes to "win-win" Pareto-optimal changes from the inherited *status quo*. "Offset rights" to pollute the neighbourhoods of the poor are granted today to those whose claim to the privilege is their history of polluting. The political basis of these "offset rights" (licences to pollute) being currently created shines forth unmistakeably.

     b. Privatization is dominated by giveaways and resultant "Rent-seeking", which warps allocation.

Another thing libertarian philosophers must paper over is the rent-seeking that occurs in the creation of private tenures. They avidly push privatization as The Panacea, but ignore the process of privatization and its consequences. Private tenure is often granted under customs that make it a prize for occupying or fixing some capital on land, and continuing to operate it with "due diligence" ("use it or lose it"). Premature investment, settlement and development are frequent results, seriously distorting the allocation of land, labour and capital and contributing to the "Congested Frontier" problem (cf. B-2.)

Some assets that are privatized in this way, *de jure* or *de facto*, include

England's North Sea oil (where it is called "performance bidding"); water in the 17 western States of the USA, and four western provinces of Canada; the radio spectrum; licenses to pollute air ("offset rights"); US farmland under Squatters' Rights (1841) and the Homestead Act (1862); US and Canadian railroad land grants; fishing quotas; farm production and acreage quotas; cartel shares; utility franchises with duty-to-serve; etc.

The tolerance of neo-classically-trained libertarian economists for such distortions knows no bounds nor shame. A current example in California is their push to convert conditional water licenses into permanent property rights. They would give the present licensees perpetual, alienable property not just in the water, but in past and ongoing government subsidies to build and operate the water distribution system.[25]

B-2. Much land remains untenured

Access to land is open by nature until and unless land is appropriated, defended, bounded and policed. No one claims land by right of production; no producer must be rewarded to evoke and maintain the supply; and submarginal land is not worth policing, unless to preempt it for its possible future values, or to preclude anticipated competition for markets or labour. Centuries of human customs have developed around regulating common use of lands with open access.

Tenure control of some land tends to drive the excluded population to untenured land (the "commons"), creating an allocational bias unless all land is either tenured or common. Thomas N. Carver styled this the phenomenon of "The Congested Frontier", and he might have added backwoods. Land which is partly common today includes parks and public beaches, streets and highways, water surfaces, wild fish and game, and some at least of the "wide open spaces" in less hospitable regions. Today there are homeless people for whom life would literally be impossible without some form of access, however precarious, to untenured land. Some of it, ironically, is near the centres of large cities, where the price of land is highest.

No great damage is done if submarginal land is untenured: it won't be used anyway. There may be damage, however, when rentable land is untenured. It attracts too many entrepreneurs with too much labour and capital, leading either to the use of private force to establish tenure - unjust, dangerous, and wasteful - or overcrowding and waste, called the "dissipation of rent," when the average cost of the average firm equals the average product of labour and capital. Fisheries and open range are classic cases.

Some land of high value is untenured or underpriced because consumers resist paying for what they think of as "free" because it has no cost of production, and which nature continues to supply even though the price is too low to ration the land economically. Examples: water whose natural source is in southern California (it is tenured, but underpriced); city streets for movement and parking space, even in New York; air and water used for waste disposal in populated areas; housing that is subject to rent controls; popular beaches and trails; oil and gas subject to field price controls; and so on.

When land is open to public access, so may be the capital used to improve it, e.g. paving of rights-of-way. Such capital may also suffer the excessive congestion. This open access to capital is mainly an incident to the lack of land tenure - a characteristic more of land than of capital as such.[26] Remember, capital occupies space, but land *is* space.

It is also possible to legislate and subsidize open access to some kinds of labour and capital services, e.g. public health measures, and education. These differ from common lands in that they are not open "by nature," but by art and public expenditure.

B-3. Landownership imparts superior bargaining power
Labour starves, in contests of endurance; land endures. A landowner is also a person with labour power. He or she can earn income like any worker. Landownership gives income above that, which gives discretionary spending or waiting power.

In contests with capital, land has the greater waiting power because over time capital depreciates, while land appreciates. Thus landowners (when free of heavy taxation) are noted for their patience. Patience is the essence of bargaining power.

Because land is fixed, more ownership by one person or group means less ownership by others. To expand is to preempt, unavoidably. Thus, the expanding agent necessarily weakens others by the same stroke that strengthens himself. Landownership often gives market power in the sale of specific commodities and services. See B-11.

B-4. Land Rent does not evoke production, thrift or investment
Land rent, however high, does not raise the rate of return (ROR) on investment in land purchase. It may sometimes lower ROR in the formation of true capital.

    a. Land rent does not determine interest rates.

There is a worldwide market for capital, flawed to be sure, but quite operational. Capital flows tend to create a common, worldwide and industrywide rate of return on capital, based on the productivity of capital as demand and the urge to consume as a limit on supply. With this the rent of land has nothing to do, directly. There is no rate of return on creating land; no common level of land rents. Higher rents do not increase the return on investments and pull up interest rates; they are capitalized into higher land values, using the given interest rate which is determined by the supply of and demand for capital, not land.

If the return to capital rises in a place or an industry, capital flows in until the rate of return on new investment falls to the common level. The excess returns to capital are competed away. When land rents rise, on the other hand, the excess returns are concealed by higher land prices which are treated as costs of production. Arbitrage pushes up land prices, using the interest rate borrowed from the market for capital where it is determined. This creates an illusion of a return that results from buying land, but acquiring land does not build the asset that yields the return. The return comes first, and exists regardless of what is paid for it; the price derives from the return (cf. A-4).

In terms of ordinary cost theory, land price is part of Fixed Cost. As demand rises, average fixed cost rises enough to soak up all excess returns. As it is sometimes put, land's "cost" is not price-determining, but price-determined. Calling it a "cost," and lumping it with other costs, has tended to hide this difference in obscurity, ambiguity, and a touch of mystery, which are the basic tools of sophistry.

If land rents do affect interest rates it is not by increasing the productivity of and demand for capital. It is likely to be the reverse: high asking prices for land can cut into and reduce the return to capital. In short, high building prices raise the demand for investment; high land values lower it.

Whether high land values do or not reduce returns to investors depends on whether they are properly high — i.e. they reflect the high productive value of land — or overpriced, in a cost-push phenomenon. Overpushing building rentals does happen, but vacancies result and correction is likely, especially when the building is on the steep gradient of its depreciation and obsolescence curves.

Overpricing land titles is common - witness all the vacant land in and around cities. It may go on for years before it is recognized and corrected, especially when land is on the steep gradient of its appreciation curve, and near an edge or ecotone (zones of change of land use) of conversion to higher use. Ordinary theory obscures this, to the extent that it treats land at all, by calling land rent a "residual." Landowners in real life are not so passive: they get paid up front when they sell to builders. (Demanding high ground rents in long term leases to builders is also common and has similar effects.) When this occurs it lowers the rate of return on building. Where the land is paid or contracted for up front and on fixed terms, the building only gets the residual.

b. Existence of land value actually lowers saving rates.

i) Land value substitutes for real capital in portfolios and thus lowers the need to create real capital. This is the same effect that historians have noted about the negative effect of slavery on capital formation. High land values may also affect interest rates indirectly by reducing saving and the supply of capital. The existence of high land rents and values, like the ownership of slaves, tends to satisfy the need for accumulation of assets without any actual capital formation.

ii) Rising land prices are net income to individuals. Most of net income is normally consumed. "Equity withdrawal" is a common form that this takes. Another form is letting land appreciation substitute for a capital consumption allowance as capital depreciates.

c. Investing in land is macro-economically sterile. It creates neither income nor capital. Socially, it is a wash: one buys, one sells, nothing else happens.

d. Public policy needs to promote capital formation but not land creation.

For creating land, thrift is not needed, nor can it avail: no man can create land. Thrift creates no land, and the value of land, however high, stimulates no thrift. Land rent may be taxed heavily without discouraging capital formation. Indeed capital formation would be encouraged if land prices were lowered, because there is a diminishing marginal utility of assets to private holders. The loss of land values would stimulate new saving to make up the loss.

e. Land price is unrelated to cost of producing land.

The present value of land is not derived from nor caused by nor related to its cost of production. It has none. Present value is derived solely by discounting future ground rents.

With capital the sequence is that persons save to form capital, a lump sum, which then yields a service flow. Capital formation precedes and causes the service flow. With land the sequence is reversed. The service flow is a free gift which simply exists. The buyer does not create it, nor cause others to create it; he simply acquires it. The expected service flow is then converted into a lump sum present value by the process called "capitalizing," i.e. making land superficially resemble capital for purposes of exchange. However, it is land price that adjusts to a given rent, rather than rent being determined at a level sufficient to reward producing the asset. The interest (or capitalization) rate at which rent is converted to price is determined by the supply of and demand for real capital, not land.

B-5. Land rent is a taxable surplus

Land rent is nearly identical with taxable surplus. This follows from the simple observation that the supplies of labour and capital are highly elastic. E.R.G. Seligman has alleged that a marginal community, on no-rent land, would have no tax base if it could tax nothing but land. In fact, this hypothetical community has no tax base anyway. Whatever labour or capital it tries to tax will leave, or never arrive. It just barely pays to use marginal land. Capital will only appear to pay a tax if it can shift it to land in the form of a lower rent on purchase price. If rent was already zero, there is no place to shift it.

This matter is treated at length in my contribution to *Private Property and Public Finance*, a volume in this series.

B-6. Uniformity in taxation between land and capital is not neutral

a. Land and capital are not interchangeable. They are mutually exclusive. Individuals may exchange one for the other but that does not change the quantity of either.

The fact of non-convertibility gives a new meaning to the ordinary concept that "uniformity" in taxation is neutral and desirable in all cases. Uniformity is desirable to avoid "excise tax" effects, but that end does not require uniformity between land and capital, only uniformity within each class.

However much the capital be taxed, it will not be converted into land. By definition, it cannot be. Likewise, however much land be taxed, it cannot be converted into capital.

It follows that "uniformity in taxation" only has merit within each class, not among them. The ideas that we should tax all income uniformly, or all property uniformly, have no merit from an efficiency standpoint.

Many State constitutions are perverse in this regard, allowing discrimination among uses of land, but not between land and capital.[27]

b. Taxing capital is non-neutral *per se.*

Heavy taxation of capital in an open jurisdiction will abort marginal investments and thus lower the intensity of all land use. It will thus distort the allocation of capital among jurisdictions, driving it away from the taxing jurisdiction, generally to its disadvantage. It will also favour less intensive land uses within the taxing jurisdiction. The effect of a property tax based on the value of capital is the same as a rise in the rate of interest. The rule is, "If a tax varies with the use to which land is put, it is biased for the use more lightly taxed."

Putting it in substitution terms, taxing capital induces substituting land for capital. This occurs simply because capital is taxed, however, and not because it is taxed more than land. It occurs whether land is taxed at a higher rate, the same rate, or no rate at all.

For neutrality, the rule then is to avoid taxing anything except land. Non-uniform taxation is necessary to avoid taxing capital, and thus to avoid non-neutrality. The ordinary argument for uniformity gets it backwards.

c. It is impossible to tax capital uniformly.

The points (a) and (b) are the stronger because capital is never taxed uniformly anyway, and cannot be. No jurisdiction even tries to include personal consumer durables in the tax base, notably excepting cars in some states. Most states exempt all personal property; some exempt large parts of it. Personal property is concealable, movable before assessment dates, and generally impossible to treat uniformly. Exempting all personal property is no solution: it opens a wide bias against things bolted to the floor, as well as against floors themselves, and walls and roofs.

The only way to tax capital uniformly is to exempt it all. The way to exempt it all, without going completely anarchist, is to raise the rate on land, which can be assessed uniformly.

d. It is impossible and undesirable to tax consumption uniformly.

What are pushed today as taxes on "consumption" exempt land-consumption. Sales taxes and VATs in practice tax many things in cascade, and others not at all. They bear on capital formation in human form, and exempt consumption of land's time-slots. To call them what they are, they are taxes on exchange, and the necessities of the poor, the middling, and parents of all levels struggling to create and maintain human capital.

B-7. Land values are hypersensitive to discount rates

The sensitivity of present values to discount rates increases as the value being discounted is further in the future. Land values are discounted from more remote future values than are values of most capital, even most durable and "fixed" capital. Consider land yielding an expected constant cash flow: let the interest rate double and the present value is halved. Compare the present value of a steer to be slaughtered in one year: let the interest rate double from 5% to 10% and the present value drops from .95 of slaughter value to .91.[28] Even that overstates it a lot because we haven't accounted for the feed bill, but never mind, the point should be clear.

Let buyers expect land's cash flow to rise annually by a growth coefficient, G, and the valuation formula is cash flow divided by the interest rate minus the growth rate (I-G), rather than I alone. Now let the interest rate double, and the present value is cut to less than half.

Or let land be yielding a nominal current cash flow and to be held in anticipation of a higher use to begin 10 years down the road, and thirty years after that to be renewed for an even higher use. Let there be a whiff of oil, or the floating value of a shopping centre, or the possible extension of a freeway and a new water supply paid by others. Let there be a fear (or hope) that Washington will debauch the currency sometime again in this century, or that another Howard Jarvis will cut land taxes some more, or that future building costs will fall: any and all of these, which are common and familiar expectations, make present values of land more sensitive to discount rates than in the simple basic capitalization model which is based on assumed constant cash flow in perpetuity.

Expectations like those denoted above by G, or like the anticipated higher future use referred to, are "a state of the public mind" (Richard Hurd, *Principles of City Land Values*). They are incapable of proof or disproof in the present and, whether proven true or false in the future, will have lost relevance, to be replaced by new expectations of new futures that unfold endlessly as time passes.

B-8. Land markets are dominated by access to long-term credit
Individual bidding power is hypersensitive to one's Internal Interest Rate (IIR). This follows from B-7.

a. Financing purchase ranges from difficult to impossible.

Few assets are priced so high as land, relative to cash flow. Financing a purchase of land therefore presents an unusually high credit barrier to the builder, new businessman or hopeful homeowner. Cash flow is seldom adequate to cover interest on a full loan, let alone the principal. The buyer must find the excess elsewhere. A poor credit rating raises the interest rate and increases the difficulties. Even a middling credit rating is not good enough to open entry to most businesses, and a weak one excludes a large minority from homeownership.

b. Land purchase is not self-liquidating.

Because market agents expect land to last forever they price it accordingly, high enough so the net cash flow just covers interest on the price, with nothing left over to pay for the principal. Thus the land buyer will never normally (or "in equilibrium") pay for it from its own cash flow, as he will pay for capital assets. The debtor will never retire the loan from the cash flow of the land, but only from other saving, or from new windfalls not expected at time of purchase. A new buyer with no equity, therefore, is a bad credit risk and gets short shrift at the bank.

c. The corollary of high land price is high carrying cost relative to cash flow.

Carrying cost is interest on the price of land. It varies with one's internal interest rate (IIR). For those with high IIRs, the carrying cost of land normally exceeds cash flow. Otherwise put, cash flow from land seldom covers carrying cost, while cash flow from depreciable capital covers more than its carrying cost because it normally has to be priced low enough for cash flow to cover both interest and depreciation. As to inventories of rising assets like steers or timber, they are like zero-coupon bonds: there is no cash flow before sale, but the famine leads to a feast of total recovery.

Since land lasts forever while demands for land grow, the normal expectation over long periods is that ground rents will rise. Present land value includes the discounted values of expected higher future rents. This makes current land values very high relative to current cash flows, which are less than expected future flows. In stock market terms, the Price-earnings ratio of land is high, like that of a growth stock. This is more than an analogy, since a large share of the assets of corporations consist of land. In the USA, corporations are the major landholders.

d. Credit barriers are barriers to equimarginal allocation of land.

Those of poor credit ratings are peculiarly handicapped in the market for land titles. This is because the carrying cost of land is interest, and because there is a structure of interest rates based on borrowers' credit ratings.

Because of the difference in carrying cost the financially strong add land to their holdings to a lower margin of productivity than prevails on holdings of the financially weak, whether we measure productivity in cash flow or service flow. This is a factor independent of and in addition to the fact that the financially strong likely place a higher current value on service flows (i.e. the amenities of land) of given objective quality.

It is often reinforced in practice, too, by the greater political power that accompanies financial strength. The combination of factors may lead the land market far away from anything approaching an efficient equimarginal allocation of land among competing firms and households, to such a degree that traditional micro theory loses much of its explanatory power and the market becomes a travesty of the Platonic ideal in the textbook.

B-9. Control of land gravitates to financially "strong hands"

a. Landownership accretes around existing nuclei.

Few people can invest heavily in an asset of high price and deferred yields. Those who can do so have a field with fewer competitors than most, and tend to expand widely. As a rustic Nebraska land economist twanged to me and others 30 years ago, "When a rancher buys these days it ain't the

quarters roundin' out, it's the sections gobblin' the quarters."[29]
One reason for that is that land is the basis for extending credit. The "sections" go to the banks for accommodation to buy the "quarters." As Prof. Rainer Schikele, the former Chief Economist of the FAO, wrote, "The basis of credit is not marginal productivity, but collateral security."

A major factor giving one a good credit rating is the prior ownership of land. Thus, those already holding title to land have access to more land at a lower carrying cost than those trying to enter the market from poverty. The result is a tendency for land to agglomerate in the hands of the financially strong (cf. B-8).

Just why some should want to expand so much as to be "alone in the midst of the earth" has puzzled many more gentler souls than Isaiah. Thorstein Veblen never turned his acidic irony to better account than in his last book, *Absentee Ownership*, describing acquisition for acquisition's sake:

> Subtraction is the aim of this pioneer cupidity, not production; ... being in no way related quantitatively to a person's workmanlike powers or to his tangible performance, it has no 'saturation point'.
>
> "Their passion for acquisition has driven them ... ; their slavery has been not to an imperative bent of workmanship and human service, but to an indefinitely extensible cupidity ...[which] is one of those 'higher wants of man' which the economists have found to be 'indefinitely extensible', and like other spiritual needs it is self-authenticating, its own voucher.
>
> "The Latin phrase is *auri sacra* [30] *fames* (fanatical lust for gold), ... They [the Romans] had reached a realization of the essentially sacramental virtue of this indefinitely extensible need of more; ... The object of this 'higher want of man' is no longer [gold], but some form of [certificate] which conveys title to a run of free income; and it can accordingly have no 'saturation point', even in fancy, inasmuch as [certificates of title are] also indefinitely extensible and stand in no quantitative relation to tangible fact....
>
> "They have always, ... wanted something more than their ... share of the soil; not because they were driven by a felt need of doing more than their fair share of work ..., but with a view to ...getting a little something for nothing in allowing their holdings to be turned to account, ..."
>
> T. Veblen, *Absentee Ownership*, 1923, pp. 138-40.

As Veblen taught, what is true of Nebraska sections and quarters is equally true of giant and small world corporations. The worldwide mergermania of the insatiable '80s followed the same pattern. Beneath the corporate veil, most corporations are large collections of real estate: industrial, commercial, agricultural, mineral, transportation, communications, and utility real estate.

    b. It follows that landownership is highly concentrated.

Land is a major basis, probably *the* major basis of the concentration of wealth. Political distribution, if egalitarian, may stave this off for a considerable time. There is also evidence that heavy land taxation, where that is applied, motivates subdivision. However, experience is that, in the absence of heavy taxation, the surplus of rent attracts absentee investors, and large concentrations reconstitute themselves inexorably. The writer and others have documented such concentration elsewhere.[31]

    What concentration means for bargaining power has been foreshadowed in B-3. What it means for market power is treated in B-11.

B-10. Land markets are sticky

Land sellers, compared to sellers of other factors, are too weakly motivated to make very efficient markets. In the basic sense, the land market is efficient if it guides land to its highest and best use, yielding the most economic rent. Time was when that would go without saying, but the semantic cleansing of theory has muddled it up. I do not use "efficient market" in the tautological sense of some rational-expectations theorists, wherein markets are efficient almost by definition because all agents are assumed to know what they are doing, and outside observers are not allowed to question it. Neither do I use efficient in the arbitrage sense, where a land market is called efficient if individual buyers of land make a reasonable return compared with their alternatives.[32] I am looking at basic social efficiency. There are many reasons why land markets fail.

    a. Weak seller motivation.

The services of land perish with time. This is a strong social reason for seeing that land is well used. It is also a private motivation which makes the market work, such as it does. If we looked only at this factor in isolation, we would infer that land markets work well.

Land is similar in this respect to capital. But capital also suffers from depreciation, obsolescence, spoilage, theft, and vandalism, and requires outlays for maintenance, protection, insurance and storage. Labour services also perish with time, when labour is unemployed; but unemployed labour also starves. Thus seller motivation is much higher for labour and capital than for land.

    b. Waiting for Godot.

Some of land's current service flow may be put into storage, for example if the land is growing timber or young fruit trees. In this, land is not unique. The service flow of the capital in the trees is similarly "plowed back" into the growing capital.

But the flow of land service may also be stored in a way peculiar to itself. Landholders may defer permanent improvements while land "ripens" into a higher use, higher enough to repay with interest the loss of one or more years' rent flow.

Strenuous efforts are made by some economic theorists to rationalize land withholding on these grounds. "Rational expectations" theorists have developed a paradigm wherein any investment decision is presumed rational and socially benign, to know all is to forgive all, and the burden of proof is on anyone who questions an individual landowner's behaviour. Whether that kind of rationalization will long succeed, or whether widespread "holding for the rise" will again be recognized as evidence of market failure, there is no doubt that it occurs on a grand scale, and much land is thus held back from current use.[33]

Withholding is also rationalized as waiting for greater certainty. This involves a fairly transparent fallacy of composition (although it seems to be opaque to those economists who make much of this point). The waiting landholder imposes uncertainty on others who are waiting to see what he will do, and of course *vice versa*, such that uncertainty motivates waiting, and waiting generates more uncertainty, in a vicious "positive feedback loop".

Waiting landholders collectively also impose costs on the public, which has at the very least a prior investment in national appropriation and defence of the land, and usually heavy investments in public infrastructure which await private response. It is a situation where the gains of waiting accrue to the private landholder but the costs accrue to others, a clear condition for market failure.

    c. Limited competition.

There is no new supply of land, as there is of capital due to current capital formation (cf. A-3). It was for this reason that Adam Smith and other classical economists called landholding a "monopoly". They did not mean there was just one owner or seller, but referred to the absence and impossibility of new supplies. They referred to a return, rent, in excess of costs needed to induce production. They referred to the fact that entry of competitors is limited to the holders of the given supply. Some moderns belittle the classicals for using monopoly in a different sense than what has become customary long after their funerals, but such an anachronism is patently unfair. They knew what they were saying.

Land rent is not wiped out by competition. Instead, it is imputed away, silently disappearing into "Fixed Cost". Higher demand for land in general evokes no supply response: rather, it simply raises the whole structure of rents. There is usually increased supply of the gross produce or service from land owing to more intensive use, but it comes from the same land. The additional output results from increments of labour and capital applied to the same land. Cf. B-4.

d. Lags in reallocation.

There is a sort of supply response to increased demand for one use of land, and reduced demand for another, because land use can be changed in response to a new structure of rents. Many micro theorists, focusing narrowly on economics as "the allocation of limited resources among competing ends," advance this to aver that land is as mobile as capital. However, reallocating land has tight limits. It is uncommonly slow because land is mostly committed to existing uses, encumbered with durable capital specialized to the existing use, and as yet not fully depreciated. Only a fraction of the potential change occurs in one year. In addition, potential reallocation is often limited by the spatial fixity or other qualitative peculiarity of specific lands. Tundra and Alpine meadow cannot be converted to the loams and warm climate of the corn belt; Utica cannot move to Manhattan, nor Death Valley to Newport Beach. The essence of land value is location; it is not easily duplicated, and of course totally stationary, by definition.

The most favourable case for supply response is where the growing use is of high value and the shrinking one of no value, as with a city growing out into a desert. Here the change of land use is even tantamount to increasing the aggregate supply, it is said or implied by some Chicago School theorists.

One problem with such a model is that deserts do not spawn great cities: even Denver, Phoenix, Albuquerque, Salt Lake City and Los Angeles all developed in oases of intensive farming. As cities spread they destroy part of what they serve and what serves them, and the reverberations ripple out vastly. Land boundaries are common and interdependent, so a change in one ecotone entails "repacking" entire regions, a long, sticky, disruptive process indeed. Expanding cities send out shock waves into the surrounding farms that travel through the entire hierarchy of farm land uses, as higher uses displace lower uses, from market gardens down to sheep grazing. Even grazing is not the lowest use: it then pushes on forestry and recreation where it finally meets the wrath of the Sierra Club (with headquarters in downtown San Francisco and offices in Washington, D.C.). Growing cities also destroy part of the natural beauty that many people value so highly that they devote their lives to protecting it.

e. Lack of homogeneous land.

Las Vegas, not a typical city, is the largest I know of that indeed grows in worthless desert. Here another factor stands out clearly: new lands are peripheral and only imperfect, partial substitutes for central land. The city must range farther for water, power, waste disposal, raw materials and markets.

The high marginal cost of adding to spreading cities, and the low true net value of the additions, are concealed, in our culture, by an elaborate and pervasive system of subsidies and cross-subsidies built into our institutions and political power structures. These drain the old centres to feed the fringes. In a systemwide accounting we find the true social cost of urban sprawl as we know it today to exceed the gains at the margins. We are not so much adding land to cities as wasting capital, dissipating central rents to do it. Thus the private rent gradient and resulting land-value gradient that we observe in the marketplace is much flatter than the true gradient that is hidden under the subsidies. Even so, the visible gradient remains impressive: values rise to $2,000/psf in San Francisco, Chicago and Manhattan, and $25,000/psf in Tokyo.

Land of rare and limited qualities is often the basis of market control: retail sites, rights-of-way, rare ores, water rights, are familiar examples. Even land of less rare qualities is often used for market control. American farm output is controlled by means of acreage limitations; Texas and now

OPEC oil production by oil well allocation of quotas based on oil reserves; and so on.

f. Lack of turnover.

Now consider the market for land titles. This is the more relevant market for the construction industry, transfering land between uses, and changing parcel sizes. If the market for land services is slow, the market for land titles is viscous. There is no flow of supply, none at all. There is no real turnover in the sense of producing and using up. There is only ownership turnover: the market only transfers existing titles.[34] (There is a supplemental market in long leases, not addressed here.)

There are few highly motivated sellers comparable to sellers of spoiling produce and obsolescing computers and vehicles. Median home-owners are motivated, when for occupational reasons they have to transfer to another region. Few other land sellers come close to that degree of motivation (and the median home represents more capital than land). Capital depreciates; goods spoil and obsolesce; idle labour starves; but land silently rises in value.

The aggregate of all land changes hands slowly, with one or two percent turnover of ownership annually (measuring the stock by value, not number of parcels — smaller, cheaper parcels turn faster). But buyers often need adjacent land, or land in particular districts or with particular qualities, and find little or no land on the market, or land controlled by one seller.

The slow ownership turnover cited above applies to total real estate, i.e. land including any buildings on it. Ownership turnover is even slower for bare land. If the average building lasts 50 years, only 2% of the land is available for re-use in any given year. Only a fraction of that 2% is for sale; the rest is renewed by the same owner. Whoever wants to buy available land in any particular area is unlikely to be faced with the "many sellers" premised by the competitive model.

g. Hoarding for vertical integration.

A common precaution against sticky markets is buying excess land for possible future expansion. This behaviour makes markets that much more sticky. It is one of those things that necessitates and justifies itself, considered in the aggregate: it is self-aggravating and self-authenticating. When anyone buys and holds for his own future expansion, everyone has to: it is a positive feedback loop of possessiveness run wild.

The composite result of individuals buying for future contingent need is that the market in raw land is turned to glue. It ceases to serve the median person in time of need. The effect is a species of vertical integration and, like all vertical integration, it destroys the free market in raw materials and vastly inflates the aggregate need for holding raw materials. This is because the pooling effect that is otherwise provided by the market is neutralized. For example, the grocer obtains, stores and keeps a wide variety of food and sundries on tap for thousands of customers. Lacking a grocer, each customer would have to maintain her own stores, and the aggregate required would far exceed that in the common grocery store. A good land market would likewise keep land on tap for the contingent needs of all, greatly lowering aggregate needs.

h. Assembly.

In certain ecotones (zones of change of land use) the technical need is to assemble small parcels into larger ones, as where commerce, industry and high rise are moving into a district of single homes on small lots. This condition maximizes market failure. It normally takes years to assemble an optimal parcel: one holdout can spoil years of negotiating and financing.

Straw buyers and front men are used to keep principals and their intentions secret. Speculators are everywhere, trying to assemble large plots or hold up other buyers. Whole districts are held by anonymous absentees; buildings deteriorate, neighbourhoods lose their natural leaders and stabilizers, and communities disintegrate leaving slums and blight, crime and arson, public charges and vandalism.

The sum of those factors makes for an inefficient market in land titles. Everyone who can tries to acquire land for his own future expansion. Timely subdivision may be foregone in anticipation of future assembly problems, skipping an entire generation of optimal land use. Neighbours adjusting lot lines have only each other to deal with. Aggregate landownership is highly concentrated because of the small numbers who can invest for deferred yields; the number of sellers in one district or for one use is more narrowly limited because of spatial immobility and low turnover and impossibility of new land creation. Financing is especially difficult because the asset is not self-liquidating. Many holders are waiting for the rise, and/ or for greater certainty to be provided by the advance commitments of others who are in turn waiting for them. Net result: wasted, underutilized land.

i. Institutional stickiness.

Land is traditionally subject to a host of legal and customary limits on use and ownership. Covenants are found in land titles: seldom in titles to cars or canned goods. Divided ownership is common, there is so much in the bundle we call land that can be owned separately. There are easements through, air rights over, mineral rights under, and neighbours and zoning all around any parcel of land. Changing lot lines is unavoidably a social process, there is no other way.

A large share of the more valuable land in cities is held by estates. Public and non-profit holders are preferentially tax exempt and often without any visible motive to economize. Water licenses are held subject to "use it or lose it" traditions leading to appalling waste. Broadcasting/telecasting licenses are highly political. And so on. Only a resource with the characteristics of land could be subject to such a wide range of non-economic pressures.

B-11. Land is a major basis of market power
We have seen that landownership conveys superior bargaining power, accretes around existing nuclei (B-9,a), and is highly concentrated (B-9,b). We have seen markets are sticky. It follows that landownership is a natural basis of market power.

a. Expansion is zero-sum.

Amassing land is always done, can only be done, by shrinking the holdings of others. To expand is to preempt. If A is to have more then B, C, D *et al.* must have less, there is no other way. A can amass more capital by saving, creating new capital, leaving B, C, D *et al.* with as much as before. A can increase his labour income by working longer, or harder, or smarter, producing more, leaving others with as much as before. He and she together can also spawn more children: labour, like capital, is reproducible, and indefinitely augmentable. Possessing land, however, means just one thing: displacing others.

In the region of the mind, the thing possessed may be shared by all with no diminution to anyone. No one's pleasure in Shakespeare, or Beethoven, or understanding physics is any less because at the same time millions of others have the same pleasure. Art, letters and science are the common property of mankind, open to all who care to acquire them. The creative producer's pleasure is in proportion to the number with whom he shares. The gratification is from sharing, not excluding. The contrast with landholding is nearly total.[35]

Amassing claims on wealth by creating and producing is not, therefore, a threat to others. Amassing capital through saving does not weaken or impoverish others. Producing goods does not interfere with others doing the same. One producer may drive another from a particular limited market, but glutting one market increases real demand for the products of other markets, and raises the real value of others' incomes by lowering prices. Amassing land, however, has to deprive others, both relatively and absolutely. Concentrated holding and control of land, therefore, have always been threats to the well-being of those left out.

Conversely, the only way the landless, e.g. in South Africa, can get land is from those who now have it. "Growth" is often advanced as the solution to maldistribution, injustice and poverty, but that is mere temporizing because land does not grow. When production and demand grow, land rents rise. Of land it is starkly true, "the problem is not production, but distribution". There is no production; only distribution.

b. Land is a natural base for monopoly and monopsony.

Massed control of land is the most natural base for monopolizing markets because land is limited. Buying land always does double duty: when A expands he *ipso facto* preempts opportunities from B. For example, a chain of service stations with most of the best corners in a town has market power, the more so if it also holds a large share of oil sources, of refinery sites, of "offset rights" to pollute air, transmission rights of way, harbour sites, and other such limited lands.

Preemption is not always just a by-product of expansion; it may be the main point of a business strategy. For example, in 1993 Builders' Emporium, a large chain of California hardware stores with large parking lots in good locations, closed down and sold out. The sites were bought up by a grocery chain. According to news reports, the stores remain empty today; the land idle. The purpose is to keep the sites from Ralph's, a competing grocery chain.

The social purpose and rationale for private property and land markets is to get land into its best use. When preemption overrides use, market failure is total; private property is discredited.

c. The differentiation of land is permanent.

If monopoly were based simply on owning a particular form of capital, all the other capital in the world could be converted into the monopolized form each time it is liquidated and the proceeds are reinvested. The same is not true of land, whose specialized qualities are permanent (see A-3 and B-10).

Land with differentiated special qualities is fixed, e.g. land in the City of London; or land suitable for growing macadamia nuts, or unloading ocean vessels, or relaying radio signals; or residential land within a superior high school district, or with ocean views and breezes. Substitution is generally possible but only at higher costs, resulting in rent gradients out from the best locations. This phenomenon is well studied and associated with the names of Von Thünen, Ricardo, and many modern location theorists.

This quality makes land a natural basis for oligopoly control of markets, or attempts at control. Land bearing certain minerals, like diamonds or oil, is fixed and limited, in spite of new discoveries and technologies. Sites most suitable for refining oil are limited: they must be near markets, with access to cheap water transport and pipelines, with "offset rights" to pollute air, with "ancient rights" to endanger or downgrade surrounding residential lands and occasionally spill oil, with access to rails and a freeway system and a labour pool, with vast backlots for tank farms, inside supportive political jurisdictions, and so on.

The fixity of land also lends itself to stability of association among oligopolists. People come and go; capital turns over, flows in and out; corporations, partnerships and syndicates are collapsed, merged, refinanced, bankrupted and reorganized. Land remains: it is always in the same place, unmistakeably identifiable and findable. It is the permanent, underlying resource whose control is always the objective of the shuffling and agitating and strife above it. Its owners, whoever they may be, will reliably join and support the local employers' association and their respective trade associations.

d. Local market power.

Tip O'Neil, the former Speaker of the US Congress, was often quoted that "All politics is local politics." One might say the same of market power.

Some lands are sold or leased with covenants against competition, as Gimbel's Department Store holds a covenant on a lot adjoining its parent store on 3rd Street and Wisconsin Avenue, Milwaukee. Such anti-competitive arrangements, however blatant, are intra-state, and apparently immune from sanctions under US Federal anti-trust laws. Scholars of industrial organization, many of them doing outstanding work otherwise, pay these grass-roots matters little heed. Researchers and activists concentrate on commodity markets at national and world levels - the ones subject to Federal sanctions, such as they are. They could probably find more severe and blatant market failure in local land markets.

Bargaining power increases with the number of options one has. A large landowner with a chain of holdings in different jurisdictions is positioned to bargain, to play off one against the other. Thus, the Disney Corporation, 1991-93, considered rebuilding and expanding Disneyland at its current site in Anaheim, or in Long Beach where it had tenure over another suitable site. Using this leverage it won concessions from both cities, "finally" choosing to expand in Anaheim.

Likewise, land is a basis for oligopsony power in local labour markets. A city's labour pool is often faced with a local employers' association whose membership is limited by the amount of industrial land within reach of the labour pool. Migrant farm labour is faced with statewide employers' associations who have the advantages of limited numbers, wealth, ancient roots and stability. Labour unions that organize a local plant are faced with the threat of the "runaway shop", or merely reallocating work among plants, when the employer owns plants elsewhere.

Custom has dulled us to it, but a corporation is a pool of separate individual landowners bargaining in concert. A century ago, corporations and limited liability were viewed with suspicion and apprehension. Today, hundreds and thousands of separate landowners pool their corporate strength against labour as a matter of course. Some employees bargain through unions, but not as a matter of course, and hardly ever with international options. In the US, less than 20% of the labour force is unionized, yet many, probably most economists treat labour as the only threatening monopoly. They see corporations as benign; a prime cause carried by many economists today is to eliminate the corporate income tax completely. Would we saw such support for eliminating the payroll tax, the most obvious cause of unemployment.

e. Land is the basis of cartels.

There is too much farmland to permit monopoly control through private action. However, production controls are exerted through public action and force of law. These controls operate through control of land, by limiting the allowable acreage in certain crops. Seldom is there any attempt to control other farming inputs like labour, fertilizer, farm capital or pesticides.

The best-known world cartel, OPEC, also works through control of a natural resource. It is important in its own right, obviously, but only one of a whole genus that it represents so conspicuously. There is a tendency for cartels to overexpand under the price umbrella they support, and then collapse, taking with them a lot of wasted capital. The effect of short-run monopoly may thus be long-run instability (cf. B-17). Either way, the effects are harmful and impoverishing.

f. Land puts the lock on monopoly.

A monopoly that limits output to raise price, or a monopsony that limits hiring, both throw workers on the street, and release other resources too. Why do not these workers and these raw materials combine in new firms? The monopoly would defeat itself if they could. Clearly the monopoly must dominate. Land is the most likely one, because of limited supply and non-reproduceability. Somehow, ordinary micro "price theory" never addresses this question.[36] It is crippled by the absence of one leg: land.

B-12. Land income is much greater than the current cash flow

a. Appreciation is current income.

The income of depreciable capital is cash flow less depreciation. The income of appreciable land is cash flow plus appreciation. That is quite a difference.

With land held for appreciation there is no cash flow to disclose the high values and the steady accrual of gains in wealth. This quality of "silent accrual" is found in land surrounding cities, or growing retail centres, as well as in land considered potentially mineral-bearing. Other land is valued for expected higher future cash flows in its present use, or some higher use to come. Some land is valued for future "plottage" increments from assembly, or "negative plottage" from subdividing.

Professors Haig and Simons have given their names to the standard definition of income which includes unrealized appreciation of durable assets like land and corporate shares as current income. Stock brokers and real estate brokers habitually do the same thing for the trade. They may appear to question it when lobbying for tax breaks, at which time some say it is "double taxation" to tax both current cash flow and appreciation. When selling stock or real estate, however, unrealized appreciation is unequivocally touted as current income, and correctly so.

Some even deny that appreciation should be taxable income at all. Yet, no one denies that depreciation should be a deduction from current taxable income. This asymmetry and glaring contradiction generally passes unremarked. It could only survive if never challenged in the profession, which apparently it is not. "Land," with its tendency to appreciate, is not in the abridged lexicon.

b. Landowning yields large non-cash service flows.

Land income also includes service flows other than cash. Because of its versatility, and fundamental character, land often yields service flows in kind that never pass through the market place. For example, land used for homes and owner-recreation yields no cash flow at all, but has high value.

It is common for economists to write of the "imputed income of durable consumer capital", especially owner-occupied houses, and occasionally to persuade some political candidate to advocate including their imputed income in the income tax base, or at least to end the deduction of interest and property taxes paid on house values. Those making such proposals, unfortunately, fail to exercise reasonable care in distinguishing houses from land. Much or most of the non-cash service flow received from consumer capital proper is not income at all, but two other things: a return from operation, maintenance, and upkeep; and a return of capital. Depreciation and expenses offset more than half the service flow from most owner-occupied houses, especially middle-aged buildings on the steep slope of the depreciation curve. The service flow from land, on the other hand, is pure income.

The measure of this imputed land income is not subjective nor fuzzy. It is interest on the market price of the land, a measure of its opportunity cost (cf. B-14 and A-2). Alternatively, it is the periodic ground rent on comparable lands. This could easily be included in the base of the present income tax, converting it in one stroke into a national land tax.[37]

Forest land yields cash only once in decades. Some land is valued mainly for ancillary benefits like the preferential access it gives to adjoining lands for grazing, recreation, water rights, waste disposal, information gleaned from mining, etc. Other land is held for its contingency value, for example for possible future expansion. Some is held preemptively to freeze out competition, and some is used (under current US income tax laws) to yield non-cash tax shelter benefits.

Part of farmland value is an amenity, especially of course in pleasant places. The value of lands held for the owner's recreational pleasure is non-cash. Part of the value of media ownership — especially through control of the radio spectrum — is power and prestige. Business sites in Newport Beach give access to water recreation; in Cambridge, Mass., to intellectual stimulus and hobnobbing. The list of non-cash service flows from land is much longer. The 15th Earl of Derby put it like this in 1881:

> The objects which men aim at when they become possessed of land in the British Isles may, I think, be enumerated as follows: (1) political influence; (2) social importance, founded on territorial possession, the most visible and unmistakable form of wealth; (3) power exercised over tenantry; the pleasure of managing, directing and improving the estate itself; (4) residential enjoyment, including what is called sport; (5) the money return — the rent.

In Ireland, during rent wars, boycotts, etc., landlords "had long decided that Ireland would yield few of the spiritual delights of land ownership." This resulted in lower prices for Irish than English land.[38]

    c. Land income is a prior claim, not a "residual." Cf. A-14.

    d. Land income is a large share of national income.

Throughout history the prime business of national governments has been to gain and keep land, mainly by force and threats (cf. B-1). The prime business of politics has been to apportion lands among the winners. A third business is then to subsidize them in various ways. It is most inconsistent, then, when the winners of all three battles counter tax proposals by pleading poverty, saying their land has little value. How little value it has may be gauged by playing "what if?" What if the English, with all their capital, were removed to Antarctica? What would be their national income?

Less drastically, we might just ask what the owners would sell England for? A common way to trivialize land values is to play "what if" the owners tried to sell it all at once.[39] What if, instead, we went to buy it all? Much of it has been off the market for centuries, with reservation prices effectively infinite. More generally, this question is addressed in detail in my contribution to a sequel in this series, *Private Property and Public Finance*.

B-13. Consuming land means pre-empting its time

To consume most goods and services is to use them up. Land is not used up. "Consuming" land must have some other meaning, therefore, than the intuitive and common idea that consuming means turning-to-waste. To consume land is rather to preempt its service flow without impairing its substance. To consume land is to occupy it for a time-slot, which may be as brief as beating a red light or (rarely) as long as the pyramids last.[40] After us life goes on, on the land once left to us which we then leave to others. "Time-sharing" was not invented by the holiday industry but is inherent in the nature of land and life.

How shall we measure land-consumption by owners, where no rent is paid? Is it purely subjective? Does it vary with the owner's mood and health? It is simpler than that, and fully practicable. The essence of consuming land is preempting the time-slot from others. Thus, holding land without using it, or using it below capacity, is a form of consumption. The measure is the market opportunity cost of land, i.e. the price times the interest rate.

Holding an urban site has been likened to holding a reserved seat at a play, sporting event, or concert. The ticketholder properly helps pay for the event, whether or not he is there to enjoy it. As a result, very few paid customers fail to show up. Likewise, people who pay cash rent for land seldom leave it vacant. Doubtless if people paid regular cash taxes to hold land, they, too, would consume (preempt) less.

Proponents of "consumer taxation" almost universally overlook this point. I am not aware of one who has proposed including land-consumption in the tax base. Aaron and Galper, propounding a "cash-flow tax," explicitly allow for letting each succeeding owner to write off the purchase of land as a cost of production, effectively exempting land rents from taxation 100%.

Theirs, and other proposals, and consumer taxes actually imposed now and in the past, bear heavily on the necessities of median families. We deride the salt tax of the French *ancien régime*, and of pre-Ghandian India. We recognize them as instruments of tyranny and class warfare, even as we tolerate modern legislators who impose comparable burdens on ourselves and economists who rationalize such taxes by belittling the necessities of life.

Doing so, they compound the deception in the label "consumer taxation". Much of what is taxed in the name of taxing consumers is actually used for capital formation: human capital formation. The same economists who say human beings are or contain capital, turn around and tell us to tax the formation and maintenance of such capital, by calling it "consumption". Coupling this with their proposed exemption of land-consumption we have the ultimate victory and application of semantic cleansing. Inconstancy, thy name is neo-classical economist?

B-14. Land's rent is its opportunity cost, regardless of use

This means land rent is a much larger share of national income than national accounts presently show.

Land income is a prior claim to the joint product of combined resources. As noted in B-13, to consume land economically is merely to preempt a time-slot from others, regardless of what one does with it. The unreaped harvests of idle land flow like water wasting through a desert into a salt sea. Lost water may sometimes be useful downstream; lost time never returns. To keep others from using a time-slot is to consume it.

A great deal of land in fact is not allocated to its highest and best use. The value of preempting this land is the highest and best use that might have been made of the land preempted. That is the economic cost. The land is not responsible if the manager fails to realize its value at optimal capacity. Neither are the persons who are excluded. Only the preemptor is responsible, as a manager. This person is the residual imputee who deserves credit for performing above par and blame for falling below.

Most economic theorizing has failed to bring out this point. The tendency is to treat ground rent as a residual, a waste basket for all the errors and dereliction of responsible economic actors. Too many economists who make much of "choice" and "opportunity cost", fail to apply that properly to land, when estimating its value. This has resulted in greatly understating the value of land relative to other factors of production. Institutional and social factors, too, often obscure the opportunity cost of land.

This is a case where theorizing lags behind practice. In dividing value between land and a building affixed to it the standard practice of appraisers, and speculative buyers too, is the "building-residual method." The land is appraised as though vacant; the building gets the remaining value, if any. The building, once attached to a specific site, loses the mobility of place and form that fluid capital possesses and has no opportunity cost but scrap value, which is often negative. Land, always lacking mobility of place, retains mobility of reuse because of its versatility, permanence, and irreproduceable location.

B-15. Land value is hypersensitive to the environment
Because of fixed location land value reflects its surroundings. Good and bad spillover values lodge in land rents because they are locational and the affected land cannot escape the bad, nor avoid sharing the good.

C

Land-driven Booms and Busts

C-1. Land value is used as the basis of credit and money

During a land boom, financial institutions lend freely on land. After a while, mortgages secured by real estate (either directly or through the corporate veil) become the major asset of banks. Credit follows collateral, and then helps boost its collateral value in a positive feedback loop. In periods of high and rising land prices, borrowers get used to pledging land to secure loans, and lenders get used to demanding it.

The credit is often used to buy still more land, to reserve for possible future use and at the same time to withhold from competitors. Such concentration and market control form the ugly side of extant western "capitalism", when enterprise degenerates into greed and acquisitions supplant innovations.

The basis of credit is not marginal productivity but collateral security. Lenders are concerned not with the productive use of their loans, but with the security provided by borrowers' ownership of old wealth.[41]

As Keynes put it in his *General Theory*, there are two kinds of risks: investment risk proper, and lender's risk. Investment risk depends on the productivity of new capital; "lenders' risk" depends on borrowers' old collateral, like land. The social purpose of investing is to create capital; the individual purpose is to buy income with security. The second purpose leads lenders to lend to the rich in preference to those who are productive. The principles are at odds; the productivity principle is clearly better from the viewpoint of basic micro efficiency.

The marginal productivity basis of lending is also better in terms of macro stability. Flows of credit dominated by cycles in the land market are highly unstable. The savings and loan industry calamity in the US in the 1980s exemplifies and should settle the point. It has many precedents, going back at least to the golden age of Florentine banking, the Dutch Tulip Bubble of 1634 and the French-English Mississippi and South Sea Bubbles of 1720. The rule has been that following each collapse the hung-over lenders woke up penitent. Reacting to the excesses they adopted something like the English Banking School philosophy of avoiding real estate loans and sticking with self-liquidating commercial loans, only to fall off the wagon in the next land boom thereby helping to repeat the cycle. How easily one generation forgets the hard lessons life taught the one before. "When will they ever learn?"[42]

C-2. Land valuation is subjective

The value of durable capital is based on expected future cash flow, and so is that of land, but there are at least three big differences. The future of most capital is short; that of land is infinite. The future of most capital is limited to the specialized use for which it was built; that of land is varied and unpredictable. The future cash flow of capital is limited by potential competition from new capital with a known cost of production; that from land is limited only by future demand and is likely to rise. It is "a state of the public mind" (Richard Hurd).

As to allocation of land it gravitates not just to the financially strong but to the psychologically susceptible, that is those most prone to overestimate future incomes, for whatever reason.

There is too little in objective reality to limit expectations. Many buyers have little understanding of valuation theory. Loan officers should be better trained than naive new buyers, but the recent history of US and Japanese banking suggests otherwise. Without understanding, there is little basis for pricing other than the behaviour of other buyers and sellers, i.e. the rest of the herd. By then valuation is purely circular and loses its anchor in reality. The history of land values, accordingly, is one of manic-depressive mob psychology with swings of high amplitude.

Suppose one decides to consult a professional real estate appraiser, to make sure he does not overbid. What do appraisers do? They locate comparable properties that have sold recently, and advise you accordingly. The buyers of those other properties hired appraisers who did the same thing. If there is a building it is different. Your valuer tells you it is not worth more than its reproduction cost, a known figure in the trade. With land, however, value is based mainly on what others are paying, i.e. the general opinion. Everyone is setting his watch by everyone else's.

There is one important party whose following of the herd will actually restrain the herd, and temper its excesses. This party is the assessor of land taxes. If land assessments rise with a herd mania, land taxes will also rise, which dashes freezing water on the mania and stabilizes the market. Here is compensatory fiscal policy in the best and original sense. This can really work. It did work in the Progressive Era, 1900-17, when reliance on property taxes was at an all-time high in the US. The major crash that was "due" in 1913 or so never happened. Several factors were at work, but this was clearly a major one.[43]

C-3. Land markets are prime causes of instability

a. Land prices move in cycles of high amplitude.

b. Investors respond to high land-price by forming land-saving capital, i.e. substituting capital for land. It is useful to distinguish five forms this substitution takes (cf. A-6, where these points are outlined).

i) Land-saving capital, like high buildings. Land-saving comprises intensification of use of previously rentable lands, or "exploiting the intensive margin of production".

ii) Land-enhancing capital, meaning capital used to improve land for a new, higher use. This includes bringing marginal land into production, on remote frontiers. However, that is only a small part of what it means. Both country and city are marked by many edges or ecotones where lower uses give way to higher uses.[44] Each is an economic frontier. Thus, land-enhancing also means converting rangeland to plowland, dryland to irrigated land, irrigated pasture to horticulture, and furrow irrigation to drip irrigation. In urban growth, it means converting farmland or wasteland to dwelling units, low-density estates to subdivisions, single-family detached units to garden apartments, garden apartments to high-rise apartments, residential to commercial, and obsolete structures to modern ones.

Developing submarginal land is particularly capital-intensive, and the payoff is notably slow. A generic example is reforesting land that is high, cold, dry and sloping, where the timber does not ripen for over a century.

iii) Land-linking capital, like canals and rails and city streets.

iv) Land-capturing (rent-seeking) capital, like squatters' improvements, and canal and rail lines built to secure land grants, and dams and canals built to secure water rights. These land-seizing investments are never optimal for society, and they always waste capital. Land-seizing investments are laid out by self-seeking individuals ("rational economic agents") with no expectation of ever recovering the capital invested because the payoff comes as title to land, which never wears out. Canal, rail, traction, water supply, freeway and other such promoters are always mainly in the business of selling lands.

v) Rent-leading capital. In urban growth, an example is over-improving land today, expecting higher demand tomorrow. This is "forcing the future". It occurs because there are "economies of simultaneity" in building. It is hardly ever economical to add stories to buildings one at a time. If you are going to build to four stories, you have to do it all at once. Suppose today's demand is high enough to justify a two-storey building, but you see the demand rising steadily over the 60-year life of the building. You build a four-storey building today, and absorb early losses on the upper two stories, as an investment for future years. A city builds a four-lane street, where two would do today, anticipating higher future usage. It puts excess capacity in its water and sewer lines, for future growth. Such examples are legion.

Economies of simultaneity are related to economies of scale. Building higher, taken by itself, suffers diseconomies, also known as increasing costs. On the other hand, building larger, with horizontal expansion, evinces economies of scale. It also requires more land, meaning more land rent. It comes into style during periods of rent-leading capital building.

In a speculative land boom, land prices go prematurely high. Premature high land values profoundly distort the character of capital investment. High land prices stimulate land-saving, land-enhancing and land-linking investments. This is a rational economic response when and if the market is sending the right signals. Ideally, an optimally high level of land rents and values serves as a community synchronizer, causing everyone to build as though others were going to build complementarily in synchronised fashion.

However, in the frenzy of a speculative boom the market sends the wrong signals. Land is peculiarly subject to irrational speculative pricing in booms because of its subjective pricing - see B-16.

Overpricing of land reserves land for two contrasting kinds of buyers and holders.

Type A buyers would "force the future" with "rent-leading" buildings. They plan to and do develop land for a future demand higher than present demand. In Chicago, 1835, this was exemplified by building four-storey buildings outside The Loop (the city centre). Overpricing and consequent over-improvement gets greater, the further out you go.

When that demand fails to materialize, Type A buyers cannot recover their money. They cannot rent out all their floor space, if that is what they built. Or they cannot use the full capacity of their tannery, harbour, shipyard, sawmill, packing plant, soap factory, brickyard, or whatever they overbuilt.

When Type A buyers develop land beyond the reach of existing infrastructure, they force extensions of same which are often losers, but they are cross-subsidized by the whole system.

Type B landowners just hold land unused or underused. Rather than force the future, they would free-ride on the future. They are usually looking or expecting to sell for a rise. Type B-1 is the aggressive outside buyer, the stereotypical "land speculator" who does this calculatingly, cold-heartedly, as a purely pecuniary investment. Type B-2 is the ancient owner whose land just happens to lie in the way of growth. Type B-2 owners are sympathetic figures in popular drama and sentiment. They are passive victims of change, clinging to old values against mechanistic, impersonal, exogenous, amoral, modernizing forces. However, their market behaviour has much the same economic consequences as that of Type B-1. Many turn out to be ambivalent, resisting change for a few years while quietly expecting to sell out for the highest price for their retirement.

The land of Type B landowners absorbs no capital directly, but much capital indirectly, by forcing the stretching-out of all land-linking investments in space, and generating no traffic or use to justify those that are built to and past them. Empty land also generates no synergistic spillover gains to raise the cash flow of surrounding, complementary lands. Thus it helps freeze capital sunk in improving them.

    c. Land-saving capital is well above average in durability. Following an argument developed by Smith, Ricardo, Mill, Wicksell, Spiethoff,

Hayek, and others, an excess commitment of capital to fixed forms with slow recovery rates brings on a shortage of job-making investing. See the summary in Haberler, *Prosperity and Depression*.

SUMMARY

In summary, we have reviewed the primary reasons why economic theory should treat land as a distinctive factor of production; and the practical inferences therefrom. Making land markets, land policy, and land taxation work well for the general welfare is a major challenge for economists and statesmen. They have neglected it for too long by swallowing the peculiar neo-classical sophisms that would obscure or deny all distinctions between land and capital.

References

1. Land is absolutely limitational. Capital is nearly so in practice: we need not dwell on rare cases to the contrary.
2. Careers both inside and outside academia are much influenced by "deep lobbying," as described by William Greider, 1992, *Who Shall Tell the People?*, pp. 42-59. "Deep lobbying" is targeting public opinion several years in the future, by building allies in think tanks, academia, the media, and select activist groups. Greider gives as an example the effort of polluting interests to undo the Superfund law. They chose The Conservation Foundation, engineering the selection of William. K. Reilly as environmental czar. Greider emphasizes the role of economists, *et al.*, as hired guns. The eagerness of many college professors and administrators to get grants at any price must be experienced to be believed, but I can attest from personal observation that it drives much of the profession and its attitudes.
3. So help me, in 1993 I saw and heard a one-factor model presented, in all solemnity. Labour was the one factor. Other economists attending saw nothing wrong: they gravely admired the model's "elegance."
4. See any standard text in micro-economics. It would be invidious to pick on any one.
5. Most of the Austrians themselves treated of capital without reference to land, as though trees grew floating in space. Two notable exceptions were Wieser, and the "Swedish Austrian" Knut Wicksell.
6. It is ironic that economists purport or affect to ape the methods of physics,

when they delete both space and time from their subject. If they have borrowed from physics, they have taken the form without the substance.

7. "Something there is that does not love a wall, that sends the frozen groundswell under it, and spills the upper boulders in the sun." Robert Frost, "Mending Wall."

8. M. Gaffney, 1994, "The Taxable Capacity of Land." Albany Law School.

9. M. Gaffney, 1967, *Extractive Resources and Taxation*. Madison: University of Wisconsin Press. M. Gaffney, 1965, "Soil Depletion and Land Rent," *National Resources Journal* 4(3):537-57.

10. Extractive natural resources are used up by consumption. Some even call them "natural capital," but that is pushing it: one resemblance does not make an identity. Land has many characteristics; permanence (which characterizes site) is only one of these. Because of the natural origin and limited stock, the exhaustion of some resources causes the appreciation of others to replace them. Thus, exhaustible resources *in situ*, before they are extracted, go through a long period of price appreciation, distinguishing them from most man-made capital. Owing to the conservation of matter, many resources are not used up in consumption, but are recyclable and recycled.

11. An example on a social scale is the bonding imposed on nuclear generators by the US Federal Energy Regulatory Commission (FERC). FERC requires utility firms to set aside a percentage of their fuel budget in a sinking fund to pay for "decommissioning" plants at the end of their economic lives.

12. The careful but captious reader is reminded that our unqualified indicatives refer to land as site. We have set aside extractive resources for special treatment (cf. n.10 above).

13. Some renewable land resources move: air, water, wild fish and game. The observations here need modifying or explicating to apply fully to them. Movable water, for example, springs from a watershed or aquifer that is fixed in space.

14. The Spanish terms for real estate are *bienes inmuebles* and *bienes raices* (rooted goods). French distinguishes land and capital: *immeubles* refers more to improvements and fixtures; *propriete fonciere* applies more specifically to pure land. German, too, has a separate term for improvements and fixtures, *unbewegliche Eigentum* (immovable property), while real estate is *Grundeigentum*, obviously stressing ground alone. In English the etymology may reveal the king's underlying ownership: "real estate" probably springs from royal estate, "real" being either contracted from "regal," or borrowed from the French and Spanish real, royal. Spanish law does recognize "regalian" ownership of subsurface minerals. (In Latin American history this

took the form of a 20% severance tax.) Our word "realize," meaning convert to money, likely derives from the fact that money was issued by kings and bore their images. The Spanish real was a silver coin of wide currency. Spanish coin was the western world's hard money for four centuries.

15. On the point, I recommend the writings of Knut Wicksell, e.g. *Value, Capital, and Rent.* After praising the works of Boehm-Bawerk, Wicksell faults him for treating capital simply as stored labour. Wicksell makes it also stored land, whose distinctiveness and importance he recognizes.

16. The Indians of America are loath to alienate tribal lands precisely to preclude improvident liquidation.

16a. Clarke, J.B., 1899. *The Distribution of Wealth*, New York: Macmillan. Wickstead, Phillip, 1914. *The Scope and Method of Political Economy.* E.G. 24: 1-23.

17. A classic study of this matter is W.I. Myers, 1920, *An Economic Study of Farm Layout.* Ithaca: Cornell University Press. It is indicative of the later neglect of land economics that one must go back so far to find the classic.

18. A recent application of the Physiocratic law is by David Bradford, *et al., National Tax Journal*, Dec. 1992, applying it to New Jersey.

19. J.S. Mill, *Principles*, "Influence of the Progress of Industry and Population on Rents, Profits and Wages," Article 4.

20. An old limerick puts it well. "A captious economist planned to live without access to land. He nearly succeeded, but found that he needed food, water, and somewhere to stand."

21. It has been suggested that satellites and space stations work without land but of course they are launched and powered and controlled and supplied from the earth. Every one to date makes extensive use of the radio spectrum, a scarce bit of economic land. Even a dead satellite uses an orbit, and one of these days there will be interference — already there is talk of star wars, and the crowded skies. It has further been advanced that micro-chips and such use so little land that land is irrelevant. This overlooks that these items are made and assembled and used in plants that spread out and produce toxic wastes, by people who arrive in autos riding over rights-of-way from homes on residential lots. Land prices in Silicon Valley are so high, and space so tight, that plants long since began moving in search of cheaper land in northern Sonoma County, Sacramento County, etc.

22. We do not address here to what extent "human capital" blurs the distinction of land and capital. We do note that economists who would "tax consumption" by taxing the formation and maintenance of human capital, while exempting the consumption of land, are involved in massive contradictions.

23. Gene pools may remain distinctive over generations, partially limiting interchangeability. We will not try to settle here the perennial quarrel of heredity vs. environment.

24. It is also ignored by most of those who call themselves "Austrians" after the great Austrian economists of the 19th Century (although one of these, Wieser, made much of the difference between land and capital, and even Hayek criticized Frank Knight for seeking to obliterate any distinction).

25. This is heavily documented in M. Gaffney, *"Whose Water? Ours."* 1922. In Polly Byer (ed.), *"Whose Water?"* Seattle: The University of Washington, and in *"What price water marketing?"* Working Paper, Department of Economics, University of California, Riverside, Ca.

26. The question of public restrooms is unpleasant but essential. It is a question whether to describe this as access to public capital or to the waste-disposal aspect of land, but viewed as the latter it is as undeniable a natural right as one can imagine. The late Arthur Becker was one of the few to elevate this lowly, embarrassing topic from being a subject of evasive scatological humour to the philosophical/ethical level it really deserves. A society may quickly be read, and in part judged, by its public restrooms. Consider this jointly with the matter of the homeless in crowded cities.

27. It is most likely that these provisions were adopted consciously for the overt purpose of thwarting any popular movement towards high tax rates on property. There is no cap on land tax rates that may be borne without destructive incentive effects. These constitutional provisions in effect shelter land rents behind the incentive needs of building investors.

28. More accurately that is from $1/1.05$ to $1/1.10$.

29. For those unfamiliar with the American township survey system, a "section" is 640 acres or one square mile; a "quarter" is 160 acres.

30. The Latin *sacra* means either accursed or holy, the emphasis depending presumably on whether described by a critical observer or one possessed. "Fanatical" seems to capture the double-edged meaning being relished by Veblen. It should give pause to many modern economists with their weakness for treating self-interest as The Holy Spirit.

31. "Who Owns Southern California?"; "The Property Tax is a Progressive Tax"; "Adequacy of Land as a Tax Base"; Falling Property Tax Rates and Rising Concentration"; "Whose Water? Ours"; "The Taxable Capacity of Water Resources"; and other writings. Among other writers and sources cited are the following. Sources on earlier times include George, 1871; Gates, 1978; Large Landholdings, 1919; Worster, 1985, pp. 98-111; McWilliams, 1939). Sources on more recent times include Worster, 1985, pp. 243-47, 291-302;

Villarejo, 1982; Roberts, 1971; Fellmeth, 1973, pp. 3-25, 163-80; Gottlieb and Wolt, 1977, pp. 500-509; Landownership Survey, 1946; Wilson and Clawson, 1945; Goodall, 1991; US Census of Agriculture, 1987, pp.16, 36, 84, 120.

32. This particular sophism may be traced back through Bodfish and Shannon to Charles Spahr.

33. See Kris Feder's study in *Land Speculation and the Business Cycle*, another volume in this series, and Lutz and Lutz (1951).

34. New titles are created, too, but they only transfer land from common to tenured ownership. There is no real turnover of land.

35. Paraphrased from Upton Sinclair, 1923, *The Goose Step*.

36. Students of industrial organization are less inclined to sweep it under the rug, but have generally failed to give it the importance it deserves. A notable exception was the Texas institutionalist Professor Montgomery, author of *The Brimstone Game*, but where are the Montgomerys of today?

37. In 1992 the US Congress passed an energy policy law including a provision that the worker who receives a parking space from his or her employer must pay income taxes on its imputed value in excess of $155/month. The imputed value is simply what nearby or comparable space rents for. This imputed land rent becomes taxable income, beginning with 1994 taxes. (David E. Rosenbaum, 1994, "IRS eludes parking tax law." New York Times News Service. Riverside, California, *The Press-Enterprise*, 24 Feb., p. A-12.)

38. "Ireland and the Land Act," *Nineteenth Century*, October 1881, p.474, cit. Roy Douglas, 1976, *Land People and Politics*. London: Alison and Busby, p.17.

39. Inconsistently, the very profession that accepts such trivialization is now advising Russia to do exactly that.

40. The other six "Wonders of the Ancient World" have all disappeared without a trace. Relative to land, human works are evanescent. "Like snow upon the desert's dusty face, lighting a little hour or two" they are gone.

41. Rainer Schikele, 1942, "Obstacles to Agricultural Production Expansion," *Journal of Farm Economics* 24:447-62. *In bello veritas*.

42. It would help if historians recorded the details more scrupulously and reminded the world more cogently. University of Chicago banking historians Lloyd Mints, Milton Friedman and Anna Schwartz have done much to belittle and bury the matter completely, a tribute to their influence but not their sagacity. Friedman and Schwartz' history of banking came at the right time to fulfill the wishful thinking of a generation wanting to be free of the fear that something other than human error by a few Directors of the Federal Reserve

Board brought on The Great Depression.
43. Unfortunately, assessors today are subject to strong political and social pressures to lag behind the market.
44. "Interfaces of supersession" is a polysyllabic equivalent used by land economists.

Bibliography

Aaron, Henry, and Harvey Galper, *Assessing Tax Reform*. Washington: The Brookings Institution, 1985.

Boehm-Bawerk, Eugen, 1907. *Quarterly Journal of Economics*, vol. xxi/2.

Bradford, David, et al., 1992. 'Tax Incidence in New Jersey' *National Tax Journal*, December.

California Commission on Immigration and Housing. 1919. *Large Landholdings in Southern California (A Report on), with Recommendations*. Sacramento: California State Printing Office.

Carver, Thomas N., 1915. *Essays in Social Justice*. Cambridge: Harvard University Press.

Clark, J.B., 1893. 'The Genesis of Capital' *Yale Review*, Nov., pp.302-15.

Clarke, J.B., 1907. 'Concerning the nature of capital: a reply to Dr Eugen von Boehm-Bawerk' *Quarterly Journal of Economics*, v.21, pp. 351-70, May. Transl. to German by dr. Josef Schumpeter. *Zeitschrift fur Volkerwirtschaft*, v. 16, pp. 426-40, 1907.

Douglas, Roy, 1976, *Land People & Politics: the Land Question in the U.K., 1878-1952*. London: Allison and Busby.

Feder, Kris, 1993. 'Land Speculation and Land Value Taxation' Dissertation, Temple University.

Fellmeth, Robert (ed.), 1971. *Power and Land in California*. Washington: Center for Study of Responsive Law.

Fellmeth, Robert, 1973. *Politics of Land*. NY: Grossman Publishers, pp. 3-25, 163-80.

Gaffney, Mason, 1961. 'The Unwieldy Time-dimension of Space' *AJES* 20(5): 465-81. October.

Gaffney, Mason, 1962. 'Land and Rent in Welfare Economics' in Marion Clawson, Marshall Harriss and Joseph Ackermanm (eds.) *Land Economics Research*. Baltimore: The Johns Hopkins University Press. Pp. 141-67.

Gaffney, Mason, 1965. 'Soil Depletion and Land Rent' *Natural Resources Journal* 4(3):537-57.

Gaffney, Mason, 1967. *Extractive Resources and Taxation.* Madison: University of Wisconsin Press.

Gaffney, Mason, 1970. 'Adequacy of Land as a Tax Base' in Daniel Holland (ed.), *The Assessment of land Value.* Madison: Univ. of Wisconsin Press, pp. 157-212.

Gaffney, Mason 1971. 'The Property Tax is a Progressive Tax, *Proceedings, NTA,* 64th Annual Conference, Kansas City, 1971, pp.408-26.

Gaffney, Mason, 1992. 'The Taxable Surplus in Water Resources' *Contemporary Policy Issues.*

Gaffney, Mason, 1992. 'Rising Inequality and Falling Property Tax Rates' Chapter 10 in Gene Wunderlich (ed.), *Ownership, Tenure, and Taxation of Agricultural Land.* Boulder: Westview Press.

Gaffney, Mason, 1993. 'The Taxable Capacity of Land' *Proceedings,* Conference on Land Value Taxation for New York State, January, 1993. Albany, New York: The Government Law Center, Albany Law School.

Gaffney, Mason, 1993. 'Whose Water? Ours' in Polly Dyer (ed.), *Whose Water?* Seattle: The University of Washington.

Gaffney, Mason, 1993. 'Who Owns Southern California?' Notes on concentration of landholdings, 1988 (revised, March 1990; May 10, 1991; Oct 24, 1993).

Gates, Paul, 1978. 'California Land Policy and its Historical Context: the Henry George Era' Institute of Governmental Studies, *Four Persistent Issues.* Berkeley: University of California, pp 1-30.

George, Henry, 1871. *Our Land and Land Policy.* Rpt. New York: Schalkenbach Foundation.

Goodall, Merrill, 1991. 'Property and Water Institutions in California' Draft, pp. 1-18, available from author, Claremont Graduate School, Claremont, California.

Gottlieb, Robert, and Irene Wolt, 1977. *Thinking Big.* New York: Putnam, pp. 500-09.

Gottlieb, Robert, and Peter Wiley, 1982. *Empires in the Sun.* New York: Putnam.

Gottlieb, Robert 1988. *A Life of its Own.* New York: Harcourt Brace Jovanovich, Publishers.

Greider, William, 1992. *Who Shall Tell the People?* New York: Simon and Schuster.

Haberler, Gottfried, 1937. *Prosperity and Depression.* Geneva: The League of Nations, pp. 70-75 (summary of Spiethoff, q.v.)

Hayek, Friedrich A.v., 1935-36. 'The Mythology of Capital' Rpt. in Fellner, William, and Bernard Haley (eds.), 1951, *Readings in the Theory of Income Distribution*. Selected by a Committee of the American Economic Assoiciation. Philadelphia: The Blakiston Co., pp.355-83.

Henry, John, 1994. Book-length manuscript on J.B.Clark.

Hurd, Richard, 1902. *Principles of City Land Values*. New York: Record and Guide.

Knight, Frank H., 1946. 'Capital and Interest' *Encyclopedia Brittanica*, Rpt. in Fellner, William, and Bernard Haley (eds.), 1951, *Readings in the Theory of Income Distribution*. Selected by a Committee of the American Economic Association. Philadelphia: The Blakiston Co., pp. 384-417.

Knight, Frank H. 1924, rpt. 1952. 'Some Fallacies in the Interpretation of Social Cost' in Stigler, George, and Kenneth Boulding (eds.), *Readings in Price Theory*, Selected by a Committee of the American Economic Association. Chicago: R.D. Irwin.

Knight, Frank H. 1931-36, six articles cited in Hayek, q.v., p 355.

Lutz, Friedrich, and Vera Smith Lutz, 1951. *Theory of Investment of the Firm*. Princeton University Press. Rpt. New York: Greenwood Press, 1969, pp 109-12

Marshall, Alfred, 1920, rpt. 1947. *Principles of Economics*. 8th ed. London: Macmillan.

McWilliams, Carey, 1939. 'Land Monopolization' Chap.2, *Factories in the Field*, Boston: Little, Brown and Co., pp.11-27.

Mill, J.S., 1848. *Principles of Political Economy*. Book IV, chap.III, 'Influence of the Progress of Industry and Population on Rents, Profits, and Wages' Article 4.

Mints Lloyd, 1945. *A History of Banking Theory*. Chicago: Univ. of Chicago Press.

Montgomery, Robert H., 1940. *The Brimstone Game*, New York: The Vanguard Press.

Myers, W.I., 1920. *An Economic Study of Farm Layout*. Ithaca: Cornell University Press.

Roberts, Polly, 1971. 'Power and Land in California' A summary of the Nader Report chaired by Robert Fellmeth, 1971.

Roberts, Warren, 1967. 'Mine Taxation in Developing Countries' in Gaffney, Mason (ed.), *Extractive Resources and Taxation*. Madison: University of Wisconsin Press.

Rosenbaum, David E., 1994. 'IRS Eludes Parking Tax Law' *New York Times News Service*. Riverside, California: The Press-Enterprise, 24 February, p.A-12.

Schikele, Rainer, 1942, 'Obstacles to Agricultural Production Expansion' *Journal of Farm Economics* 24:447-62.
Shannon, H.L., and H.M.Bodfish, 1929. 'Increments in Land Values in Chicago' *Journal of Land and Public Utility Economics* 5:29-47.
Sinclair, Upton, 1923. *The Goose Step, A Study of American Education*. Pasadena: Published by the author. Wholesale Distributors, The Economy Book Shop, 33 South Clark St., Chicago.
Spahr, Charles B., 1891. 'The Single Tax' *Political Science Quarterly* 6:625-34.
Spiethoff, Arthur, 1925. 'Krisen' *Handworterbuch des Staatswissenschaften*, 4th ed., Jena, vol VI, 70-86.
The Press-Enterprise, Riverside, 1993. 'Vons buys Builders' Emporium Stores', 15 October, p. C-7.
Tideman, T.Nicolaus, 1982. 'A tax on Land Value is Neutral' *National Tax Journal* 35:109-11.
Triffin, Robert, 1940. *Monopolistic Competition and General Equilibrium Theory*. Cambridge, Massachusetts: Harvard University Press.
US Census of Agriculture, 1987, pp.16, 36, 84, 120.
US Department of the Interior, Bureau of Reclamation, 1946. *Landownership Survey on Federal Reclamation Projects*. Washington: USGPO
Veblen, Thorstein, 1923. *Absentee Ownership*. New York: B.W.Huebsch.
Villarejo, Don, 1986. *How much is Enough? Federal Water Subsidies and Agriculture in California's Central Valley*. Davis: California Institute for Rural Studies, Inc.
Wicksell, Knut, 1938. *Lectures on Political Economy*, trans. E.Classen., New York: The Macmillan Co.
Wicksell, Knut, 1954. *Value, Capital, and Rent*, trans. S.H. Frowein. London: G.Allen & Unwin
Wieser, Friedrich von, 1888, trans. 1893. *Natural Value*. C.A. Malloch (trans.) London: Macmillan and Co.
Wilson, Edwin, and Marion Clawson, 1945. *Agricultural Land Ownership and Operation in the Southern San Joaquin Valley*. Berkeley: USDA, Bureau of Agricultural Economics.
Worsteer, Donald, 1985, *Rivers of Empire*. New York: Pantheon Books, pp. 98-111, 243-47, 291-302.

The Economics of Efficient Taxes on Land
Nicolaus Tideman
1

L and can be taxed in a number of different ways. It can be taxed according to its area. It can be taxed according to estimates of its sale value, as occurs under the property tax of the U.S. and other countries. It can be taxed according to estimates of its rental value. Sales of land can be taxed according to selling price, or according to the difference between selling price and the previous selling price.

This review is concerned with taxes on land that have little or no detrimental effects on economic incentives. Therefore it concentrates on taxes on land according to estimates of sale value or rental value. Taxes on land according to area discourage the use of marginal land. Taxes on land sales, whether the base is the full sale price or the increase in price since the previous sale, encourage people to hold on to land when someone else could use it more productively. These taxes are therefore excluded from this review. The review also excludes taxes on depletable minerals.

Section 2 deals with classical views of taxes on land, covering the ideas of François Quesnay, Adam Smith, David Ricardo, James Mill, John McCulloch, John Stuart Mill and Henry George, and influences and controversies among these writers. The two issues that provoked the greatest disagreement were whether it was possible to separate the value of land from the value of improvements for tax purposes and whether or to what extent a tax on land could be fair.

Section 3 deals with income effects of taxes on land. It discusses the possibility that taxes on land are partly shifted. If these effects occur, they do not constitute distortions, and they do not occur in open economies or if taxes are accompanied by benefits of corresponding value.

Section 4 is concerned with the adequacy of land as a tax base. It discusses the circumstances under which public spending will raise land rent by enough to pay for the spending.

Section 5 deals with the ethics of taxing land. In this section, three sources of land rent are identified: nature, public services, and private activities. The greatest ethical controversy arises with respect to the component of rent attributable to nature. George argued that what is provided by nature should be regarded as the common heritage of all, so that all rent from this source should be collected publicly. Those who currently have extensive land holdings have been most vocal in asserting that the imposition of such a tax would be an unjust confiscation of property. A rent-seeking perspective says that it may be better to accept the status quo than to suffer the losses from conflict that arises when the status quo is subject to challenge. A separation of constitutional from legislative choices create a forum in which advances in moral evolution can be incorporated into legal institutions without enduring all of the losses from rent-seeking conflict that would arise if existing rights had no protection from new legislation.

Section 6 summarizes the conclusions.

2
Classical Views Regarding the Taxation of Land

It is appropriate to begin a discussion of the economics of taxing land with an extensive discussion of the ideas of classical economists on the subject, because they developed many positions that can still be supported and also debated some subjects that are still controversial. A review of their positions uncovers ideas of continuing relevance and also provides insights into chains of influence.

The Physiocrats

That taxing land is a uniquely attractive way for governments to obtain revenue was one of the central tenets of the Physiocratic system developed by François Quesnay and his followers in the 1750s and 1760s. In his "General Maxims for the Government of an Agricultural Kingdom," Quesnay (1963 [1756], p. 232) says in Maxim V:

> That taxes should not be destructive or disproportionate to the mass of the nation's revenue; that their increase should follow the increase of the revenue; and that they should be laid directly on the net product of landed property, and not on men's wages, or on produce, where they would increase the cost of collection, operate to the detriment of trade, and destroy every year a portion of the nation's wealth. [Emphasis in the original.]

Quesnay's concern about taxes that "operate to the detriment of trade" corresponds to the modern concern about the dead-weight loss of taxation. What Quesnay meant by "the net product of landed property" was the return to owners of land after subtracting any money they had advanced for seeds or other inputs, that is, the rent of land. Economists from Adam Smith

105

on have acknowledged the validity of Quesnay's insight that a tax on rent, unlike a tax on almost any other base, does not "operate to the detriment of trade," that is, it has no dead-weight loss.

The Physiocrats went on to argue that, since all taxes were in the end paid out of rent, it would be sensible to replace all other taxes by a single tax on rent. However, the premise that all other taxes are in the end paid out of rent would be valid only if other inputs were supplied perfectly elastically. When other inputs have finite elasticities, taxes on them are not shifted completely to rent, and it is no longer the case that the owners of land are better off with a single tax on land. Nevertheless, one can still give the Physiocrats credit for first having the insight that taxing the rent of land is a uniquely non-destructive way for governments to obtain revenue. This idea formed part of the heritage from which all subsequent classical economists wrote about taxing land.

Adam Smith

Smith (1937 [1776], pp. 777-78) offers four maxims of taxation that were widely accepted and quoted by subsequent classical writers:

> I. The subjects of every state ought to contribute towards the support of the government, as nearly as possible, in proportion to their respective abilities; that is in proportion to the revenue they enjoy under the protection of the state. The expense of government to the individuals of a great nation, is like the expense of management to the joint tenants of a great estate, who are all obliged to contribute in proportion to their respective interests in the estate. In the observation or neglect of this maxim consists, what is called the equality or inequality of taxation. Every tax, it must be observed once for all, which falls finally upon one only of the three sorts of revenue above mentioned [rent, profit and wages], is necessarily unequal, in so far as it does not affect the other two. In the following examination of different taxes I shall seldom take much further notice of this sort of inequality, but shall, in most cases, confine my observations to that inequality which is occasioned by a particular tax falling unequally even upon that particular sort of private revenue which is affected by it.
>
> II. The tax which each individual is bound to pay ought to be certain, and not arbitrary. . . .
>
> III. Every tax ought to be levied at the time, or in the manner, in which it is most likely to be convenient for the contributor to pay it. . . .

IV. Every tax ought to be so contrived as both to take out and to keep out of the pockets of the people as little as possible, over and above what it brings into the public treasure of the state. . . .

Note that while the first clause of Smith's first maxim sounds like what a modern writer would call an ability-to-pay principle, the second clause and second sentence indicate that he might equally well be thinking of a benefits-received principle. It is reasonable to conclude that Smith did not distinguish between an ability-to-pay principle and a benefits-received principle, or consider the possibility that they might conflict. The remarks at the end of the first maxim suggest that Smith may not have considered it improper to have a tax that fell on one factor and not others.

Smith discusses separately taxes on "the rent of land," by which he means the rent of agricultural land, and taxes on "ground-rents," by which he means the rent of land under buildings. In his discussion of taxes on the rent of land, Smith notes that such a tax can be levied either according to a schedule that is fixed once and then left unaltered, or according to a schedule that is updated regularly. The land tax in England was levied in Smith's time according to a schedule that had been established about a century earlier, in the reign of William and Mary. This schedule, the product of a notional rental value of the land and a tax rate, was known to bear only a cursory relation to the true rental value of land even when it was initiated and had become even more outdated in the intervening century. Smith notes the efficiency of such a tax, saying (1937, p. 780), "As it has no tendency to diminish the quantity, it can have none to raise the price of that produce. It does not obstruct the industry of the people."

Smith says that, since rents had risen almost everywhere in the intervening century, the invariance of taxes had generally operated to the benefit of landowners. But the opposite could also have happened. Furthermore, the system had only been workable because there had been no great change in either the value of silver or the silver content of money.

Smith then takes up the case of a tax on rent that varies with every variation in rent, mentioning that the Physiocrats regarded such a tax as the most equitable of all taxes. Smith comments favorably on the practice of the Venetians of requiring all leases to be registered publicly and using these values as the basis of taxation, with "equitable estimations" and a 20% discount for land that is cultivated by those who own it. He notes that such a system can discourage owners of land from improving their land. To overcome this difficulty, he recommends that owners who are contemplating improvements be allowed to have their taxes fixed at pre-improvement levels for periods long enough to recover their investments.

Smith notes that some jurisdictions relied on systems of assessment that had reputations for being very accurate. But he doubts that governments would undertake the effort needed to keep assessments accurate, and therefore he regards systems based on recorded leases to be better.

Smith also discusses taxes proportional to what land produces, noting that these can be quite disproportional to rent and that they discourage both the improvement of land and its cultivation.

Smith's discussion of taxes on ground-rents occurs within his discussion of taxes on houses. He notes that a tax on houses is a combination of a tax on buildings, which he says is passed on to the occupiers of buildings, and a tax on ground-rent, which is paid by the owner of the land. (Smith's assertion that a tax on buildings is paid entirely by the occupiers of buildings is true only if there is a perfectly elastic supply of capital.) Smith regards ground-rent as a highly suitable base for taxation (1937, pp. 795-96):

> Ground-rents are a still more proper subject of taxation than the rent of houses. A tax upon ground-rents would not raise the rents of houses. It would fall altogether upon the owner of the ground-rent, who acts always as a monopolist, and exacts the greatest rent which can be got for the use of his ground. . . .
> Both ground-rents and the ordinary rent of land are a species of revenue which the owner, in many cases, enjoys without any care or attention of his own. Though a part of this revenue should be taken from him in order to defray the expenses of the state, no discouragement will thereby be given to any sort of industry. The annual produce of the land and labour of the society, the real wealth and revenue of the great body of the people, might be the same after such a tax as before. Ground-rents, and the ordinary rent of land, are, therefore, perhaps, the species of revenue which can best bear to have a peculiar tax imposed upon them.
> Ground-rents seem, in this respect, a more proper subject of peculiar taxation than even the ordinary rent of land. The ordinary rent of land is, in many cases, owing partly at least to the attention and good management of the landlord. A very heavy tax might discourage too much this attention

and good management. Ground-rents, so far as they exceed the ordinary rent of land, are altogether owing to the good government of the sovereign, which, by protecting the industry either of the whole people, or of the inhabitants of some particular place, enables them to pay so much more than its real value for the ground which they build their houses upon; or to make to its owner so much more than compensation for the loss which he might sustain by this use of it. Nothing can be more reasonable than that a fund which owes its existence to the good government of the state, should be taxed peculiarly, or should contribute something more than the greater part of other funds, towards the support of that government.

The remarks at the end of this passage indicate that Smith favoured a tax on ground-rents as an expression of a benefits-received principle.

David Ricardo

Ricardo's law of rent allows the rent of land to be described as the residual after paying the costs of variable factors of production. With this law, Ricardo provided a theoretical foundation for the idea that taxes on rent are a source of revenue that is particularly attractive for its lack of harmful effects on an economy. Ricardo used the law of rent as the basis for distinguishing between taxes that inhibit production and those that do not. He says (1911 [1821], p. 115):

> A land-tax, levied in proportion to the rent of land, and varying with every variation in rent, is in effect a tax on rent; and as such a tax will not apply to that land which yields no rent, nor to the produce of that capital which is employed on the land with a view to profit merely, and which never pays rent; it will not in any way affect the price of raw produce, but will fall wholly on the landlords.

Ricardo goes on to say that a tax on all cultivated land, no matter how low, will raise the price of agricultural products by causing some land to be withdrawn from production. Thus Ricardo criticizes Smith's assertion (1937, p. 788) that taxes on agricultural production are equivalent to taxes on rent and are paid by landlords. In fairness to Smith, it should be mentioned that he undoubtedly understood that a tax on agricultural production discourages improvement and cultivation. But he did not take the next step and see that this implies that it raises the price of agricultural goods, thereby shifting some of the tax from landowners to consumers.

Ricardo then criticizes Smith's claim (1937, p. 780) that, when a land tax "is assessed upon each district according to a certain invariable canon, . . . the landlord is in all cases the real contributor, . . ." Ricardo says that such a tax will cause some land to be withdrawn from production. For Ricardo's criticism to be valid, there must be some land that is taxed in excess of the rent of the land. If a historically fixed assessment happened never to exceed the rent of land, no land would be withdrawn from production, and the tax would be paid entirely by landlords. Since the land tax in England was very low, it is possible that this condition was met.

In his discussion of taxes on houses, Ricardo quotes from Smith's remarks on taxes on ground-rent and the ordinary rent of land. He then comments (1911, p. 131):

> It must be admitted that the effects of these taxes would be such as Adam Smith has described; but it would surely be very unjust to tax exclusively the revenue of any particular class of a community. The burdens of the state should be borne by all in proportion to their means: this is one of the four maxims mentioned by Adam Smith which should govern all taxation. Rent often belongs to those who, after many years of toil, have realised their gains and expended their fortunes in the purchase of land or houses; and it certainly would be an infringement of that principle which should ever be held sacred, the security of property, to subject it to unequal taxation. . . . And if it be considered that land, regarded as a fit subject for exclusive taxation, would not only be reduced in price, to compensate for the risk of that taxation, but in proportion to the indefinite nature and uncertain value of the risk would become a fit subject for speculations, partaking more of the nature of gambling than of sober trade, it will appear probable that the hands into which land would in that case be most apt to fall would be the hands of those who possess more of the qualities of the gambler than of the qualities of the sober-minded proprietor, who is likely to employ his land to the greatest advantage.

It is possible that when Ricardo wrote these words, he was thinking about his own circumstances. According to the *Encyclopedia Britannica* (1992), Ricardo, having made a fortune in the stock market, had retired to his extensive land holdings in Gloucestershire at the time that he wrote *The Principles of Political Economy and Taxation*.

Ricardo's appeal to Smith's first maxim treats it as if it is exclusively an ability-to-pay principle and neglects the part of the maxim that has a benefits-received flavour. His comments on risk make sense only if it is assumed that he is referring, not to a regime in which land is subject to a particular tax, but rather to a society in which land has come to be "regarded as a fit subject for exclusive taxation," but no action in that direction has yet been taken. In other words, Ricardo is suggesting here that, because of the consequences with respect to perceived risk, it would be harmful to an economy if people started to think that a particular tax on land would be appropriate, even without action in that direction being taken.

Ricardo did not address Smith's argument that ground-rent is a particularly suitable base for taxation because it is the result of good government.

James Mill

James Mill (1824, p. 242) repeats what had become the received wisdom about taxes on rent:

> It is sufficiently obvious, that the share of the rent of land, which may be taken to defray the expenses of the government, does not affect the industry of the country. The cultivation of the land depends upon the capitalist; . . . To him it is a matter of perfect indifference whether he pays the surplus, in the shape of rent, to an individual proprietor, or, in that of revenue, to a government collector.

He goes on to say that when European monarchs financed their governments by income from royal lands and levies on barons, all of the expense of government came from rent. In Asia, somewhat similarly, the practice of the principal monarchs had been to place levies on individual cultivators of amounts that corresponded to rent.

Mill then argues that if people were to migrate to a new country, a rule of financing government from the rent of land would be particularly attractive because "industry would not by that means sustain the smallest depression; and . . . the expense of government would be defrayed without imposing any burden upon any individual" (1824, p. 243). Since land, Mill argues, would yield more than what government would need to expend, the surplus rent might as well be disposed of by letting land be private property, subject to whatever taxes are needed to support government.

Mill (1824, pp. 244-45) then offers a version of Ricardo's argument that in existing circumstances, singling out land would be unfair:

> Where land has, however, been converted into private property, without making rent in a peculiar manner answerable for the public expenses; where it has been bought and sold upon such terms, and the expectations of individuals have been adjusted to that order of things, rent of land could not be taken to supply exclusively the wants of government, without injustice. It would be partial and unequal taxation; laying the burden of the state upon one set of individuals, and exempting the rest. It is a measure, therefore, never to be thought of by any government which would regulate its proceedings by the principles of justice.

Mill then argues that if the rent of land rises as a result of legislation, it would be proper and expedient for the legislature to appropriate the increase in rent for public purposes. Furthermore, he argues, the legislature increases rent by measures that permit population to increase. Therefore increases in rent can be subject to special taxation without injustice. Mill allows, however, that there would be practical difficulties in distinguishing between the amount of rent that had been conferred upon landowners by previous legislation and that which might properly be appropriated.

Mill next makes reference to an article on taxation, written by "M'Culloch" for the Supplement to the *Encyclopedia Britannica*. Mill describes this article as "masterly" (1824, p. 248) and says it asserts "that the whole of what the land can ever yield, is conferred, in the case supposed [when rent increases as a result of growth of a community], on the owner of the land, by the previous legislation." Mill agrees that if this premise is true, then a tax on land would be improper partial taxation of only one class. But he disputes the premise:

> The real question is, whether any thing, beyond a certain amount of annual benefit, namely, what is at present derived, with such increase as can be rationally anticipated within the number of years' purchase for which the land would sell, can, in a really equitable, excluding a merely technical, mode of considering the subject, be regarded as the property of the land-owner.

It is understandable that Mill should question the assertion that no special tax on land can ever be justified. However, Mill's proposal to allow "such increase as can be rationally anticipated within the number of years' purchase for which the land would sell" does not provide either a principled or a practical distinction between the part of rent that he regards as justly belonging to the owners of land and the part that can justly be the subject of a special tax.

John R. McCulloch

The "M'Culloch" to whom James Mill referred was presumably John R. McCulloch (born 1789; died 1864), whose treatise on taxation (1968 [1852; first edition, 1845]) discusses taxes on land in some detail. McCulloch begins his discussion of taxes on rent (1968, p. 41) with a criticism of Adam Smith: "Dr. Smith's opinion that taxes on the rent of land, taking the term in its popular and broadest sense, fall wholly on landlords, is, no doubt, an error." The reason, McCulloch says, is that rent in the sense of payments to landlords is a combination of return to land and return to capital. But it is clear that Adam Smith understood this, because he says (1937, p. 784): "The discouragement which a variable land-tax of this kind might give to the improvement of land, seems to be the most important objection which can be made to it." However, McCulloch is in any case right to emphasize the fact that payments to landlords include a return to capital as well as a return to land.

McCulloch then acknowledges that if a tax is levied only on rent, it will have no effect on the price or quantity of agricultural production and will be paid entirely by landlords. But he objects to taxes on rent on practical grounds (1968, pp. 44-45):

> In a practical point of view, taxes on the rent of land are extremely objectionable. It is, as already stated, quite impossible to separate rent into its elements, or to say how much is paid for the soil and how much for improvements. No two agriculturists ever arrive, in any case of this kind, unless by accident, at the same conclusion; and the best judges affirm that, generally speaking, the distinction is impracticable. When, therefore, a tax is laid on rent, it is necessarily proportioned to its gross amount, or to the total sum paid to the landlords, without regard to the sources whence it is derived. Inasmuch, too, as it is for the interest of all parties to conceal its amount, it is no easy matter to ascertain this gross rental. But, without laying any stress on this circumstance, a tax on rent is one of the least expedient that can be suggested. It has always been, and will unavoidably continue to be, a formidable barrier to improvements.

Then McCulloch says that even if the distinction could be made, a tax on rent would be unjust (1968, pp. 45-46):

> If direct contributions for the public service be resorted to, they should, in
> as far as possible, be universal, and proportioned to the means of all classes
> of contributors. Governments should never abandon this fundamental
> principle or yield to exaggerated and fallacious estimates of the advantages
> to be derived from laying taxes on certain classes of individuals, or
> descriptions of income. All sorts of property which have been lawfully
> acquired should be considered as equally sacred and equally entitled to
> protection. It is true, as has been stated by Mr. Ogilvie [fn: Essay on the
> Right of Property in Land, *passim*] and others, that landlords, as such, are
> not producers, but merely receivers of income which would otherwise
> belong to the state. But a right of property in land has everywhere been
> coeval with the establishment of civilized societies; and to invade it,
> whether by depriving landlords of any of the advantages fairly resulting
> form its possession, or by making them contribute more than their fair
> share to the exigencies of the state, would be barefaced oppression and
> robbery.

McCulloch goes on to dispute the idea that a new nation such as
Australia or the United States ought to retain public ownership of land and
lease it. Such a practice, he says, would discourage improvement and result
in neglect of land. The establishment of a right of private property in land,
he says, is "the grand source of civilization," inspiring love of country and
posterity.

McCulloch rails against the Physiocrats' assertion that land is the only
source of wealth, and their proposal for a single tax on land. He estimated
the gross annual rent of Great Britain and Ireland to be about £60 million
in 1848 (based on income tax returns), while public expenditures were £73
million, so that a single tax on land would not raise enough revenue to
finance government. In this calculation he appears to have taken no account
of land that was cultivated by those who owned it, or of the rental value of
urban land used for owner-occupied housing and businesses. But McCulloch
would say that this proves nothing about the possibility of financing
government from rent alone, because he believed that most of the income
of landlords was a return to capital rather than land.

McCulloch acknowledges that the British tax on land has not obstructed
improvements at all. But he believed that any increase in this tax would be

wrong (1968, pp. 56-57):

> We may regret, perhaps, that this tax was not more equally distributed, and
> its limits somewhat extended at the Revolution. But it cannot now be
> interfered with. It has been placed on its present footing for more than a
> century and a half; so that, whether it were at its establishment unwisely
> limited or unfairly assessed, has long ceased to be a matter of any practical
> importance. New rights, new interests, and new generations have grown
> up under the existing system; the lapse of time having completely obviated
> or sanctioned any defects in its original constitution. The landlords have
> long stood, in respect of taxation, on the same footing as the rest of the
> community; and can with justice be subjected to such taxes only as are laid
> on merchants, manufacturers, and other capitalists. It is obvious, therefore,
> that all projects for laying particular burdens on the land, however
> varnished or disguised, should no longer be looked upon as projects for the
> imposition of equitable taxes, but for the confiscation of a portion of the
> property of the landlords! If such flagitious schemes be ever entertained,
> they will form a precedent that will justify the repudiation of the public debt
> and the subversion of every right.

McCulloch mentions an instance in which local assessments were so
high as to cause people to abandon land. He then lumps together taxes on
rent and on the gross product of land (1968, p. 57):

> The more, indeed, that their operation is inquired into, the more clearly it
> will appear that taxes proportioned to the rent or to the nett or gross produce
> of the land are the bane of every country in which they exist.

Nevertheless, McCulloch ranks different forms of taxes on land (1968,
pp. 60-61):

> But when, despite its inequality and other bad consequences, the imposition
> of a tax on land, or on the rent of land, is determined upon, the preferable
> plan is to estimate the value of land or the rent as fairly as practicable; and
> having done so, to make the assessment perpetual at a *low* per-centage upon
> such valuation, without ever varying the latter or the rate. Variations in the
> rate are least pernicious; but all uncertainty, either as to the valuation or
> the rate, inevitably discourages the employment of capital on the land, and
> depresses the most important branch of national industry. . . .
> . . . [With respect to local taxes] the limitation of the rate is unluckily
> impracticable; but we shall do what is next best, if we declare that the

valuation on which it is to be raised shall be a perpetual *maximum;* and that though, under certain circumstances, it may be reduced, it shall not, under any circumstances, nor in any case whatever, be increased. It is, of course to be understood that this limitation of the valuation applies only to land; for it will be afterwards seen that but little, if any, inconvenience arises from varying the assessments in the case of buildings, and such like descriptions of property.

McCulloch's positions on taxing land form a fascinating combination of standard analysis, reasonable new arguments, and outrageous errors. He is correct in observing that a tax on land that exceeds rent can drive people off of land. It is also true that an anticipation of the possibility of such a tax in the future can discourage investment. But it does not follow that the best tax on land is a tax at a very low rate on assessments that can fall but not rise. Such an argument makes no allowance for the fact that the opportunity cost of not increasing the tax on land and enduring a slight risk of discouraging investment is that either some other tax with serious harmful effects will have to be raised, or public expenditures will need to fall. And it makes little sense to endorse increases in assessments on buildings while condemning increases in assessments on land on the ground that they discourage improvements.

McCulloch's comments serve as a useful reminder that the consequences of a real tax depend not on logical consequences derived by theoreticians, but rather on the expectations induced by the actual behavior of those who administer the tax. Still, it seems exceedingly narrow-minded to suppose that it is not possible to devise instructions for those who administer a land tax that will allow increases in land value due to changing external circumstances to be taxed, while excluding increases in value resulting from capital improvements. It seems particularly strange that McCulloch should be unable to imagine justification for increasing assessments when increases in land value are often due to public expenditures. Perhaps this blindness comes partly from having considered "land" to be only agricultural land and not urban land. But the seemingly blind deference to the interest of those who own land might also be traced to the fact that McCulloch was, as described by the *Dictionary of National Biography* (1917, Vol. XII, p. 463), the eldest son of the laird of Auchengool, and thus presumably the owner of a significant amount of land himself.

John Stuart Mill

In his discussion of general principles of taxation, John Stuart Mill develops a variation of his father's argument with respect to a special tax on land. He argues (1965 [1848], pp. 819-21) that the rent of land increases as a result of the progress of society, and therefore the owners of land have no just claim to this increase in their income. He proposes a valuation of all land in the country. Upon revaluation at a later time, Mill suggests that it would be possible to estimate how much of the increase in the rental value of land was due to causes other than the efforts of the owners of land, and levy a tax on this base. He argues (1965, p. 821) that in making future increments in rent subject to special taxation, "every shadow of injustice to the landlords would be obviated, if the present market-price of their land were secured to them; since that includes the present value of all future expectations."

Mill's conclusion is not justified by economic theory. If the rent of land were invariably equal to the product of its sale price and the interest rate, then one might argue that every increase in rent or in the sale price of land represented an unanticipated windfall. However, there is no reason why people should expect rent to be invariant over time. Expectations of non-constant rents are reflected in sale prices that differ from the rent divided by the interest rate. Thus one cannot in general be sure that an increase in rent and in selling price is not something that an owner of land anticipated and bargained for, leading to a rate of current return on investment that was less than the interest rate in the years preceding the realization of the rise in rent and selling price. In these circumstances, a tax on the increase in the selling price of land has the discriminatory character that Mill condemned.

There is an argument for special taxes on increases in rent, suggested by Adam Smith and James Mill, to which this objection does not apply. To the extent that increases in rent and selling price are the result of government actions, taxing the increase is a reasonably unobjectionable form of tax discrimination. An owner of land might still say, "When I bought this land, I anticipated that a bridge would be built beside it, and paid for by others. I acknowledge that I am better off having the bridge built and paying the taxes assigned to me than I would be without any bridge, but it is still unfair to require me to pay." Such an argument is unlikely to be convincing. The general principle that might be proposed is that if is permissible for society to decide to do *X* (not build a bridge), then it is permissible for society to decide to do any *Y* that makes everyone better off than with *X*.

Mill also argues (1965, pp. 821-22) that the existing land tax should be regarded not as a tax, but rather as a reservation of a part of the rent of land for the State, and therefore not a departure from the principle of equal taxation.

In his subsequent discussion of taxes on rent, Mill makes the standard argument that a tax on rent is paid entirely by landlords, provided that the return to improvements is properly excluded from the base, and that such a tax therefore has no other effects on an economy. However, he nevertheless opposes such a tax, saying (1965, p. 826), "A peculiar tax on the income of any class, not balanced by taxes on other classes, is a violation of justice, and amounts to a partial confiscation." Thus he approves only of a tax on "a portion of any future increase [in rents] arising from the mere action of natural causes." However, he argues that, "[E]ven this could not be justly done, without offering as an alternative the market price of the land."

Mill appears to be saying, in other words, that to tax increases in rent justly, one must offer to buy all land from landowners at the prices that prevail at the time from which rent increases are to be taxed. If selling prices could be determined adequately, this more restrictive position would overcome to some extent the objection raised earlier regarding anticipations of future increases in rent. It would not deal with a person who predicts accurately that his land will have a high future value that current markets do not recognize and argues that this rise in rent is a return on his investment of effort in identifying profitable opportunities that others do not see.

Henry George

Henry George first set out his views on taxing land in a pamphlet titled "Our Land and Land Policy, National and State," which he published in 1871 (George, Jr., 1960 [1900], p. 220). He elaborated his views in *Progress and Poverty* (1960 [1879]). George's primary concern was not to devise a better tax system, but rather to explain why a growing incidence of poverty accompanied the maturation of a new society, and to offer a remedy for this phenomenon. From his experience in California in the 1850s and 1860s, he saw a causal connection between the rise in rent that accompanied progress and the concurrent fall of wages (George, Jr., p.

210). He viewed this as a result of an artificial scarcity of land caused by speculators withholding land from production. The remedy that George proposed (1960, pp. 403-07) was to abolish all taxes except for a tax on land values. He argued that this would make land more accessible to those who wanted to use it productively and make land speculation unprofitable. The greater accessibility of land and removal of other taxes would raise wages and lower prices, thereby raising the standard of living of workers.

Like the economists who preceded him, George argued that taxes on land were paid entirely by land owners and did not add to costs. What distinguished George from earlier writers was that, while Ricardo, James Mill, McCulloch and John Stuart Mill regarded the concentration of taxes on land as an unjust confiscation of property, George regarded it as just and proper, rectifying the error that had been made when individuals had been allowed to appropriate rent disproportionately. George took the position (1960, p. 334) that only human effort could create a right of ownership:

> What constitutes the rightful basis of property? What is it that enables a man justly to say of a thing, "It is mine!" From what springs the sentiment which acknowledges his exclusive right as against all the world? Is it not, primarily, the right of a man to himself, to the use of his powers, to the enjoyment of the fruits of his own exertions?

George argued that, since no one made the land, people could claim only a right to the human improvements to land. All had equal rights to the value of land, which rights were properly recognized by public collection of the rental value of unimproved land from every possessor of land. However long land may have been held subject to little or no taxes, the claim of all to share in rent could properly be asserted at any time.

There is an obvious similarity between George's proposal and that of the Physiocrats. However, where George saw his proposal as one of restoring justice, the Physiocrats saw their proposal as a measure to increase the net incomes of land owners (which it would do if labor and capital were supplied perfectly elastically).

In stark contrast with McCulloch, George (1960, p. 418) held that the separation of the value of land from improvements was simple:

> Were all taxes placed upon land values, irrespective of improvements, the scheme of taxation would be so simple and clear, and public attention

would be so directed to it, that the valuation of taxation could and would be made with the same certainty that a real estate agent can determine the price a seller can get for a lot.

At the time that George wrote, the rental value of land in the U.S. was considerably greater than government spending. One of George's critics, as reported by Cord (1965, pp. 38-39), estimated in 1885 that a tax on land might produce revenues four times greater than government expenditures. George proposed leaving landowners with enough rent to give land titles some sale value (1960, p. 405), but collecting the preponderance of the rent of land whether it was needed for public purposes or not (1960, p. 406). (Using any surplus for a citizens' dividend would adequately dispose of any surplus.)

George's proposal leaves unaddressed the question of how the rent of land ought to be divided among levels of government.

Summary
The classical writers were unanimous in their agreement that a tax on land was paid entirely by the owners of land and had no detrimental effects on production, whether the tax was levied on sale value, rental value, or, like the British land tax, an arbitrary historical figure for each parcel. This conclusion was subject to the requirements that the tax be less than the rental value of the land and that the assessment procedure exclude all human improvements from the tax base. McCulloch was convinced that no such assessment procedure could be devised, George that such assessment was simple.

Ricardo said that the belief that land was suitable for special taxation would make the holding of land risky, thereby causing cultivators to be replaced by gamblers as holders of land. George said that land would tend to be held by speculators if it was not taxed. Since these propositions involve different premises, they are not contradictory.

Smith and James Mill said that land was particularly suited to special taxation when increases in land value were the result of government action. John Stuart Mill argued for a tax on all future increases in land value, provided that owners of land were given the opportunity to sell their land at the price prevailing before the tax. McCulloch regarded any taxation focused on land as unjust and inexpedient.

Smith and George saw no difficulty with respect to justice in taxing land. George asserted, in fact, that justice required it. Ricardo, James Mill, McCulloch and John Stuart Mill, on the other hand, regarded it as unjust to subject land to new special taxation. James Mill regarded the taxation of land as highly appropriate for a new country. McCulloch thought any new country should replicate the land ownership institutions of England, regarding the attachment to land as an important source of social stability. George saw the same virtue in recognizing equal claims to the value of unimproved land.

3
Consequences of Income Effects
of Taxing Land

One of the ways in which a tax on land can affect an economy is by changing the distribution of initial endowments, and hence, through income effects, changing the quantities and prices in the efficient equilibrium of the economy. A general feature of the redistribution of initial endowments that is entailed in taxing land is that resources are redistributed from the current generation to generations that have not yet been born. The current generation responds by saving more, and future generations do not respond in the short run because they have not been born yet. Nichols (1970, pp. 336-37) says:

> Taxing rents should lower the price of land and therefore the amount of capital gains on land which result from economic growth. To satisfy the same saving motives as before the tax was imposed will require an increase in the rate of capital accumulation.

The increase in savings that Nichols mentions occurs not only from the diminution of gains from holding land in a growing economy, but also from the one-time reduction in wealth from the initiation of a tax on land, even if the economy is static.

Martin Feldstein (1977) traces the effect on saving of taxing land in an overlapping generations model. In this model, a tax on land lowers the aggregate value of assets in which people can invest, which increases the demand for capital, and hence increases investment. The increased investment lowers the interest rate, which raises the value of land and thus shifts at least part of the land tax from owners of land to owners of capital. Feldstein asserts that under some not implausible values of parameters, the effect on interest rates is great enough to make owners of land better off after the tax than before. However, Chamley and Wright (1987) show that the rise in the price of land can be at most one half of the tax on land.

Feldstein emphasizes that the effects he identifies, because they operate through income effects rather than substitution effects, do not qualify as distortions. There is no deadweight loss involved. It is also noteworthy that Feldstein's model is of a closed economy. If a tax on land is implemented in a small, open economy (e.g., a single city), there would be no impact on interest rates, and the consequences that Feldstein identifies would not arise.

Feldstein (1977) also discusses an effect of land taxes that operates through risk aversion and portfolio composition. A tax on land, he says, lowers the value of land without changing its relative riskiness. With the value of land diminished, investors would not be satisfied with the large percentage of their portfolios that would be held in the form of capital, and would therefore bid up land prices, thus again shifting some of the tax. Wolfgang Eckart (1983) also discusses this effect, but adds the qualification that if the tax on land is used to finance an invariant level of expenditures, with the tax rate changing to offset any fluctuations in land prices, then there is no risk associated with the tax. The only effect of the tax is to reduce the wealth of those who own land at the time that the tax is introduced. The portfolio selection effect disappears.

Calvo *et al.* (1979) note that Feldstein's result disappears if it is assumed that people have utility for the utility of their children and therefore make bequests to them, and that the proceeds of the tax are returned to citizens in either the older or the younger generation.

The models used by Feldstein and by Calvo *et al.* have only one kind of consumer. Feldstein mentions in passing (1977, p. 350) that his results would not apply if landowners were a distinct class. It is reasonable to speculate that the strong neutrality results of Calvo *et al.* would not persist if land were held by individuals with different levels of wealth, and the proceeds of the tax were not returned to citizens in proportion to their land holdings. As Fane (1984) points out, there is nothing surprising about the conclusion that lump-sum redistributions of income alter relative prices.

Fane (1984) also explains how Calvo *et al.* could have reached the conclusion that Feldstein's model (without bequests) yields some shifting of even a compensated tax. He says that Calvo *et al.* must have had in mind a situation in which a tax is levied and the proceeds are then returned to citizens period by period. A truly compensated tax, he argues, would involve the government issuing perpetual bonds at the same time as it levied the tax, using the proceeds of the tax to pay the interest on the bonds, and using the proceeds of the bonds to make lump-sum payments to the owners of land at the time the tax was introduced. Such a scheme would have no effect on the equilibrium of the economy. Fane's truly compensated tax would also have no portfolio effect, since the bonds would substitute for land in portfolios.

The principal conclusions that can be drawn from the discussion of income effects of taxing land are that higher rates of saving can be expected and that part of the tax may be shifted. But such effects entail no inefficiency, and they do not arise if those who are taxed receive benefits corresponding to the taxes they pay. It is reasonable to conjecture that if a model along the lines of the ones discussed in this section included a labor-leisure choice as well as a consumption-saving choice, then, in addition to promoting saving, an uncompensated tax would raise output by inducing people to forego some leisure.

4

The Adequacy of Land Taxes for Financing Local Public Goods

Up to this point in the review, taxes have been considered primarily in isolation, without connection to the public services they might finance. It is as if taxes were exactions that must be tolerated, without any rationale. It might be hoped that in a democracy at least, taxes would entail a *quid pro quo* of public services that were worth at least as much as the taxes needed to pay for them.

With local public services, the ability to benefit from public spending depends on being close to the place where the spending occurs. This increases demand for land in the vicinity of places where public services are provided, raising land rents. Private production activities with marginal costs less than average costs share with public services the quality of requiring a subsidy if the efficiency of pricing at marginal cost is to be achieved. If in addition, the activity is one that, because of transportation cost or some other consideration, yields a lower benefit to those who are more distant from it, then that activity will also raise rents in the vicinity of the place where it is conducted. In recent years, economists have noted that for activities with distance-related benefits, there are interesting conditions under which the presence of an activity, whether it is a public service or a private production activity with marginal cost less than average cost, raises rent by enough to pay the difference between total cost and the sum of marginal costs at the efficient level of output. An excellent review of this literature can be found in Mieskowski and Zodrow (1989, pp. 1135-40).

The modern discussion of this subject started with Harold Hotelling, who suggested (1938, p. 242) that:

... taxes on incomes, inheritances, and the site value of land ... might well be applied to cover the fixed costs of electric power plants, water works, railroads, and other industries in which the fixed costs are large, so as to reduce to the level of marginal costs the prices charged for the services and products of these industries.

It is puzzling that Hotelling would put income taxes and inheritance taxes in the same category with taxes on the site value of land, since only the last of these has no dead-weight loss, but in any case his paper initiated the discussion of the relationship between rents and subsidies to achieve marginal-cost pricing.

The more modern literature on relationships between rent and spending on activities with distance-related benefits addresses at least three distinct questions:

1. For a given population, what happens to rent as activities vary?

2. For a given pattern of activities, what happens to the relationship between rent and subsidies as population varies?

3. When population and activities are both optimized, what is the relationship between rent and subsidies?

Smolensky *et al.* (1970) provide an analysis that bears on the first question, though they did not address it directly. They discuss the efficient size and spacing of a local public facility, in a model in which the facility has a zero marginal cost of use, housing density is uniform, all households have the same demand for the facility, and use of the facility entails a travel cost that is proportional to distance traveled, with travel possible only in two perpendicular directions. With zero marginal cost of use, efficient use requires a zero marginal payment for use. With density assumed to be invariable, financing can be provided efficiently by lump-sum charges on either households or land; the two are equivalent. Smolensky *et al.* show that efficient provision requires size and spacing of the facility such that the gross benefit of a household that is most distant from a facility, on the boundary between the areas served by two facilities, is equal to the average net benefit. Thus a system of financing that equalized net benefits would involve no payment by households on the boundary between service areas, and the net benefit of every household, after paying its assigned share of costs, would be equal to the gross benefit of households on the boundary.

The model developed by Smolensky *et al.* does not include determination of the rent of land. However, with identical consumers, differential rents must reflect variations in net benefits. Thus the collection of differential rents provides exactly the amount of money necessary to provide the efficient level of the service.

Flatters *et al.* (1974, pp. 101-02)) explore a version of the third question, the problem of choosing the population size and level of consumption of a local public good that will maximize utility of identical citizens. There are no distinctions among locations within a city in the model that Flatters *et al.* use; what offsets the ability to spread the cost of the public good among additional citizens is diminishing marginal productivity of labor. Flatters *et al.* show (1974, fn. 3, p. 102) that when the utility of citizens is maximized, "all land rents are devoted to public good production and all wage income to private goods production."

Vickrey (1977) considers an economy in which every city occupies a strip of land along a shoreline. There is more shoreline than is needed for cities, and land outside cities is assumed to have no value. The social cost of the land used by each activity is the addition to the transportation cost of the goods that are carried past the activity. Therefore if transportation cost is proportional to distance, the sum of transportation costs is equal to the total rental value of all land. Transportation cost is assumed to vary with the square of output, but this does not lead to infinitesimal plants, because larger plants permit the spreading of fixed costs. To achieve prices equal to marginal costs, firms need subsidies equal to their fixed costs. But under Vickrey's assumptions, fixed cost is equal to transportation cost when average total cost is minimized, and the sum of transportation costs is equal to the sum of land rents, so that the sum of land rents is exactly equal to the sum of the subsidies that are needed to achieve marginal cost pricing. Thus Vickrey (1977, p. 339) proposes the "GHV" (George-Hotelling-Vickrey) Theorem:

> In an economy of efficiently organized cities in a state of perfect competition with each other, the aggregate of the land rents (calculated as the marginal social cost of holding land) generated by the urban agglomeration produced by the existence of activities with economies of scale within the city will equal the subsidies required to enable these activities to sell their output at prices equal to their respective marginal costs.

Vickrey then discusses reasons for thinking that this equality between the sum of rents and the sum of subsidies that efficient firms need to achieve marginal cost pricing will persist as various special conditions he has assumed are relaxed.

Vickrey (1977, pp. 342-43) also discusses a way in which surplus rent might be eliminated by labor mobility combined with competition among cities:

> A more interesting concept would be that of a limited labour force, freely mobile among cities. Expansion of the scale of cities, and, possibly, the establishment of new cities, would lead to an increase in the demand for labour, and an increase in its wages, represented in this model by the level of the input coefficients to the labour supply activity, representing an increase in the supply of consumer goods necessary to produce a unit of labour for use in other activities in the city. Full competition among cities would, in this instance, lead (a) to the elimination of any new land rents to landlords, over and above the amounts taken to finance the fixed costs; and (b) to the transfer of this surplus, plus the additional surplus generated from the increase in efficiency to labour, at least in the case where there is no shortage of city sites and, hence, conceptually free entry for additional cities.

Arnott and Stiglitz (1979) clarify some of the logical relationships surrounding the equality of rents and public goods expenditures. An equality between rents and public goods expenditures produced by optimizing population is labeled by them the Henry George Theorem. They consider an economy of identical individuals who receive utility from lot size, a private good and a pure public good that is not congestible. Individuals are assumed to make a fixed number of trips to the center of an urban area and to have tastes such that everyone lives on a lot of unit size. Individuals compete for land which is auctioned by the government, with the proceeds of the auctions used to finance the public good and any residual divided equally among residents. Arnott and Stiglitz show that, for *any* level of spending on the public good, if the city has a population that maximizes per capita utility given that level of spending, then differential land rents will equal spending on the public good. In this case, differential land rent is the excess of rent above rent at the edge of the city. Arnott and Stiglitz then show that for an arbitrary distribution of the population with respect to some characteristic that parametrizes their utility functions and an arbitrary relative density function, as well as an arbitrary level of spending on a public good, it continues to be true that when population is optimized, the sum of differential rents is equal to spending on the public good. They note that this equality does not in general hold for an economy of multiple cities, because it is not in general possible to divide a prescribed number of people into a whole number of optimal sized cities.

The above result is achieved not by competition, but rather by population assignments by a planner. Arnott and Stiglitz (1979, p. 487) mention a working paper (Stiglitz, 1978) in which conditions under which competition achieves the planning optimum are identified. These conditions are:

    1. Costless migration;

    2. Freedom to form new cities on islands that are not scarce, with the right to exclude potential residents;

    3. An economy large enough that each person regards the utility of non-residents as exogenous;

    4. A combination of economies and diseconomies of scale resulting in optimal cities of a positive, finite size; and

    5. Homogeneous land.

Arnott and Stiglitz (1979, p. 488) summarize their results as follows:

> ... in all large, Pareto optimal spatial economies in which differential land rents are well defined, the Henry George Theorem holds. Whether the Henry George Theorem holds in a competitive economy depends on, among other things, one's view of what constitutes competitive behavior in a spatial economy.

Arnott and Stiglitz (1979, p. 488) mention that the Henry George Theorem does not hold if differential rent is not well defined, as when land rent is not uniform along the city's boundary. I would conjecture that in this case, for a city with an optimal population, spending on the public good lies between differential land rent defined relative to the minimum and maximum values of rent at the boundary of the city.

Arnott and Stiglitz distinguish the Henry George Theorem from relationships that can be derived between differential land rents and the value of local amenities for a *given* population. The Henry George Theorem specifies an equality between land rent and spending on a public good when population is such as to maximize per capita utility, in a large economy in which the spatial distribution of economic activity is Pareto optimal and differential land rents are well defined. The capacity of differences in land rents to reflect differences in the value of public services, on the other hand, is derived from an assumption of perfectly mobile individuals with identical preferences. Arnott and Stiglitz (1979, pp. 494-96) show that when individuals vary in their valuations of amenities or disamenities, land rents systematically understate the value of amenities and overstate the cost of disamenities.

Variations in preferences would not cause impacts of amenities on rent to deviate from their aggregate value if people had preferences that fit discrete types, and there were enough people of each type to fill a whole number of cities of an optimal size. Both because people are not perfectly mobile and because there is a continuum of preference types, impacts on rent do not measure aggregate value perfectly. In the long run, people get some consumer surplus not reflected in rent from valuing the services they receive more than unsuccessful bidders. In the short run, the fact that people are not perfectly mobile means that when public services change, some people will incur moving costs to obtain services more suited to their preferences, and others will endure less than optimal locations because the potential savings are less than moving costs.

Tideman (1990, p. 349) mentions a further condition that would be needed for land rents to provide a perfect measure of differences in the value of local public services: capital would need to be either perfectly mobile or not at all durable. (Capital is not incorporated in the Arnott and Stiglitz model.) As with the absence of perfect human mobility, the lack of perfect capital mobility means that the value of capital can fall (or rise, though this would be less common) because of a change in the services provided to a site.

These departures from the conditions needed for rent to reflect the value of services mean that not all efficient services can be financed by the increases in rent that they generate. They also mean that an ideal evaluation of the efficiency of a change in public services, or in a private activity receiving a public subsidy, would be based on the sum of the change in land rents, the change in the value of immobile capital, and the change in the population's "locational surplus," that is, the amounts they would pay not to have to move from the area.

5
The Ethics of Taxing Land

A simple Benthamite approach to the ethics of taxing land would say that since taxes on land have the capacity to raise revenue without harming economic incentives, and actually improve allocation in some cases, they are good. As much revenue as possible should be collected from taxes on land before other taxes are considered. It must have been precisely because they were aware of this argument that Ricardo and McCulloch gave arguments with respect to justice for not concentrating taxes on land. More complex arguments arise when the taxation of land is considered from an ethical perspective.

An examination of the ethics of taxing land must give separate consideration to three different sources of the rent of land:
1. The value attributable to nature;
2. The value attributable to public services;
3. The value attributable to private activities.

Even if it is not possible to specify how the value of a given site might be divided among these causes, the ethical evaluation of taxes on value attributable to the different sources leads to different types of taxes.

Taxes on the Value of Land Attributable to Nature
What is meant by the value of land attributable to nature is the value of agricultural land that is not near roads or towns, as well as the value that land near natural harbors and other specially attractive features would have if they were not developed.

The strongest ethical argument for a special tax on the value of land attributable to nature is George's assertion that all persons have equal rights to the gifts of nature. Opposing this argument is the assertion of Ricardo and McCulloch that because long established institutions have assigned land rights to individuals, any special tax on land is unjust. George (1960, p. 339) replies that there has never been a power capable of granting a just title of exclusive ownership of land. The vast preponderance of land titles were created by unjust coercion. Collecting taxes on land is the righting of injustice.

Careful replies to this argument are rare. More common have been such responses as the Duke of Argyle's description (quoted in George, 1946 [1892], p. 55) of George as "such a preacher of unrighteousness as the world has never seen," and his ideas as "immoral doctrines" and "profligate conclusions." In a more temperate vein, Frank Taussig (1916, p. 106) said of the movement to collect more rent for public purposes:

> Though the principles which underlie it are among the most settled in the theory of economics, they bring a shock to the common notions about the sanctity and stability of real property; and their application involves a disturbance of the common ways of dealing with real property.

George does indeed call on people to depart from a settled way of thinking. But that is not a reason to reject his ideas.

One way of bringing coherence to objection based on property rights being settled is to call on the modern theory of rent-seeking (Krueger, 1974). When entitlements can be shifted by political success, societies will waste resources on efforts to organize political coalitions. It may be better to accept an unjust arrangement than to allow the battle over entitlements to continue. But such thinking would have left us with segregated schools, unenfranchised women and slavery. Societies need an avenue by which they can give recognition to their evolving moral progress.

The rent-seeking argument can be acknowledged while still accommodating new understandings about what justice requires for entitlements. A distinction between ordinary legislation and the process of constitutional amendment serves this function. The fifth and fourteenth amendments to the U.S. Constitution forbid the taking of property without just compensation. And yet the thirteenth amendment abolished slavery and prohibited any state from compensating those who had been called the owners of slaves. These provisions are consistent with the idea that any new understanding of the requirements of justice that eliminates all of the value of some assets can be implemented only through the constitutional process, with its greater guarantees that the change truly is a new understanding and not merely a rent-seeking success (Tideman, 1988).

A different sort of response to George is offered by Murray Rothbard (1982, chs. 9-11), who agrees that all unjust seizures of land, no matter how old, should be rectified, but asserts that the first person to transform land usefully acquires a right to its use in perpetuity. This perspective at least avoids the hypocrisy that is entailed when those who have land as the result of fighting say there should be no more fighting over land. But Rothbard's ethic is unattractive in other ways (Tideman, 1991, pp. 112-13). It provides incentives for the inefficient premature development of land and leaves no route by which some of what nature provides can be preserved undisturbed, even as a private park.

Some people reply to George by bringing up a hypothetical case of an elderly widow who has no way of supporting herself except from the rent of land purchased with her husband's hard-earned money. Collection of the full rental value of land would cause her to starve. There are two ways in which this objection can be answered. First, it is widely agreed that there are social obligations to provide for those who are unable to provide for themselves. There would be a social obligation to provide for the widow in some way if she had invested all her money in companies that failed. Second, when a society discovers that it has not been recognizing the rights of some persons, the new recognition of rights must lead to losses by some persons. If the cost of the "moral accident" of failing to recognize rights is assigned to those who would have benefited from the continued failure to recognize them, then people will be motivated to think carefully about the sustainability of the claims they purchase (Tideman, 1988, p. 1720).

Another possible response to George is the assertion that those who were born well after social institutions cannot have birthrights to land because the contingencies that led to their births would not have occurred under other institutions. But such an argument could be used to justify slavery, or any mistreatment of children by parents who chose to have children for the purpose of mistreating them.

Taxes on the Value of Land Attributable to Public Services

The argument for taxing the value of land attributable to public services goes back to Adam Smith's comment (1937, p. 796) that:

> Nothing can be more reasonable than that a fund which owes its existence to the good government of the state, should be taxed peculiarly, or should contribute something more than the greater part of other funds, towards the support of that government.

To collect through taxation the addition to the rental value of land that is attributable to public services is only to require people to pay for what they receive.

If there is an ethical argument against such a tax, it would be based on the idea that the exchange is compulsory rather than voluntary. Even this argument would not be valid if people were perfectly mobile and capital were either mobile or non-durable. To put the matter another way, because people are not perfectly mobile, it is possible for some people to be made worse off by changes in public services that are financed by the increases in rent that the services produce. The possibility of moving at some cost places an upper bound on potential harm from such rent-financed services. But such an upper bound must reflect not only the monetary costs of moving, but also the loss of utility from parting with familiar territory.

The ethical reply to this is three-fold. First, if there are going to be public services, their financing will have to come from somewhere. Financing public services by taxing the increases in rent that they generate has the virtue of approximating a benefits-based financing system. Second, if there are any personal characteristics such as age that are accepted as bases for discriminating among citizens and are believed to be correlated with benefits, holding location constant, then lump-sum compensation to those who are made worse off by changes in services can be provided. It is only those whose losses are not explainable by any acceptable basis of discrimination that must endure uncompensated losses. Finally, the decision to live in a polity with others can be regarded as agreement to take one's chances with respect to the possibility that future changes in public services will not be worth as much as their tax cost. Communities can have differing rules regarding the circumstances under which public services are changed, to accommodate varying attitudes toward the risk of such losses. For these reasons, the collection of rent to finance public services stands on quite a firm ethical foundation.

Taxes on the Value of Land Attributable to Private Activities
If there is a system of paying those who undertake activities that raise land rents according to the rises in rents that are attributable to their activities, then the collection of these rent increments to finance such subsidies has the same ethical basis as the collection of rent increments generated by public activities. If there is no such system, then the ethical basis for collecting these rent increments is akin to that for taxes on the value of land attributable to nature. These increments of rent are not due to actions of the landholders, so landholders cannot justly complain if the increments are collected publicly.

Ethical Conclusion
The most difficult aspect of the ethical principles underlying social collection of the rent of land, as Taussig said, is that "they bring a shock to the common notions about the sanctity and stability of real property." The accommodation of this shock in a changed perspective is referred to among advocates of Henry George's ideas as "seeing the cat." This expression originated in a speech by Judge James G. Maguire in the late 1880s, in support of Henry George's ideas (Post, 1930, pp. 12-14).

Maguire reported an occasion when he came upon a painting in a store window that appeared to be a landscape, though a sign below it said, "Do you see the cat?" A group of people was looking at the painting, among whom one, described by another as a crank, insisted that what appeared to be a landscape was actually a cat. Maguire inquired of the crank how he could claim that the painting was a cat, and the crank replied by identifying a bird as one of the cat's ears, a twig as an eye an so on. But Maguire could still see only a poorly drawn landscape. The crank said that the space between two branches was the cat's tail. Maguire was about to say that there was no cat's tail there, when suddenly the whole cat stood out before him, and he was thereafter never able to see anything in the picture but the cat.

Thus the idea that nearly all the rent of land can and should be collected socially involves a rearrangement of perceptions into a new conception of a harmonious social order. This is the basic ethical challenge of the proposal that nearly all of the rent of land can and should be collected publicly.

6
Conclusions

Taxes on the sale value or the rental value of land are efficient in a world of perfect information because the amount of the tax that is due for any site is independent of any action that the owner of the site might take.

In conditions of imperfect information, these taxes discourage land speculation by making land unattractive to persons with extreme beliefs about the future value of land. It seems likely that this discouragement of speculation is in general efficient, although it can be inefficient if those with extreme beliefs are correct or if the tax makes it not worthwhile to acquire information that would save more in improved allocation than the cost of acquiring the information.

Taxing land also shifts land from persons with low discount rates to persons with high discount rates, mitigating capital market imperfections and probably shifting land from speculatively idle assignments to active use.

Taxing land can change the equilibrium of an economy through income effects on those who pay the tax. The general direction of such effects is to encourage more saving and, presumably, more work effort. These effects do not arise when land is taxed to provide additional public services that are worth what they cost, or if the proceeds are returned to persons who make bequests. The income effects would arise if a land tax were substituted for an income tax, because those who paid would be alive to respond, while many of those who were net beneficiaries would be unborn.

Efficient local public services (or efficiently subsidized private activities with distance-related benefits) raise surrounding land rents by enough to pay the difference between total costs and the revenue from marginal cost pricing, provided that tastes are standardized and other factors are perfectly mobile. The fact that tastes are not standardized means that some benefits will not be reflected in rents. The fact that people and capital are not perfectly mobile means that these factors are affected, generally negatively, by changes in services.

Taxes that fall solely on land raise different ethical issues, depending on whether one considers the component of rent due to nature, the component due to public services or the component due to private activities. To place a special tax on the component of rent due to public services is only to require people to pay for what they receive. If private activities are subsidized according to the rises in land rents that they engender, then these have the same ethical basis. The ethical basis of a tax on the component of rent due to nature is that people have an obligation to share the provenance of nature equally.

The research for this chapter was supported by the Lincoln Institute of Land Policy in Cambridge, Massachusetts. The Institute is a non-profit and tax-exempt educational institution established in 1974 to study and teach about land policy, including land economics and land taxation.

References

Arnott, Richard J. and Joseph E. Stiglitz, "Aggregate Land Rents, Expenditure on Public Goods, and Optimal City Size," *Quarterly Journal of Economics 93* (1979), pp. 471-500.

Bentick, Brian L. "The Impact of Taxation and Valuation Practices on the Timing and Efficiency and of Land Use," *Journal of Political Economy 87* (1979a), pp. 859-68.

"   "The Capitalization of the Property Tax and Idle Land: Comment," *Land Economics 55* (1979b), pp. 545-48.

"   "A Tax on Land May Not be Neutral," *National Tax Journal 35* (1982), p. 113.

Bourassa, Steven C. "Economic Effects of Taxes on Land, " *American Journal of Economics and Sociology 51* (1992), pp. 109-13.

Brown, Harry G. "Land Speculation and Land-Value Taxation," *Journal of Political Economy* 35 (1927), pp. 390-402.

Chamley, Christopher and Brian D. Wright. "Fiscal Incidence in an Overlapping Generations Model with a Fixed Asset," *Journal of Public Economics 32* (1987), pp. 3-24.

Calvo, Guillermo, A., Lawrence J. Kotlikoff and C. A. Rodriguez. "The Incidence of a Tax on Pure Rent: A New (?) Reason for an Old Answer," *Journal of Political Economy 87* (1979), pp. 869-74.

Comolli, Paul M. "Principles and Policy in Forrest Economics," *Bell Journal of Economics 12* (1981), pp. 300-09.

Cord, Steven. *Henry George: Dreamer or Realist?* Philadelphia: University of Pennsylvania Press, 1965.

Davenport, H.J. "Theoretical Issues in the Single Tax," *American Economic Review 7* (1917), pp. 1-30.

Dictionary of National Biography. Oxford: University Press, 1917.

Douglas, Richard W. "Site Value Taxation and the Timing of Development," *American Journal of Economics and Sociology 39* (1980), pp. 289-94.

Eckart, Wolfgang. "The Neutrality of Land Taxation in an Uncertain World," *National Tax Journal 36* (1983), pp. 237-41.

Ellson, Richard W. and R. Blaine Roberts. "'Managed' Urban Land Markets," *Public Finance Quarterly 14* (1986), pp. 466-79.

Ely, Richard T. "Land Speculation," *Journal of Farm Economics* 2 (1920), pp. 121-35.

Encyclopedia Britannica. *Micropaedia*, Vol. 10, pp. 38-39. Chicago: Encyclopedia Britannica, 1992.

Fane, George. "The Incidence of a Tax on Pure Rent: The Old Reason for the Old Answer," *Journal of Political Economy 92* (1984), pp. 329-33.

Feder, Kris. "Issues in the Theory of Land Value Taxation," Doctoral Dissertation, Temple University, 1993.

Feldstein, Martin. "The Surprising Incidence of a Tax on Pure Rent: A New Answer to an Old Question," *Journal of Political Economy 85* (1977), pp. 349-60.

Fischel, William A. "The Urbanization of Land: A Review of the National Agricultural Lands Study," *Land Economics 58* (1982), pp. 236-59.

Flatters, Frank, Vernon Henderson and Peter Mieskowski. "Public Goods, Efficiency, and Regional Fiscal Equalization," *Journal of Public Economics 3* (1974), pp. 99-112.

Gaffney, M. Mason. "Ground Rent and the Allocation of Land among Firms," in *Rent Theory: Problems and Practices.* Ed.: Frank Miller. North Central

Regional Research Publication 139 (1961), University of Missouri Research Bulletin 810, pages 30-49 and 74-82.

"   "Tax Reform to Release Land," in *Modernizing Urban Land Policy*. Ed.: Marion Clawson. Baltimore: Johns Hopkins, 1973, pp. 115-52.

George, Henry. *A Perplexed Philosopher*. New York: The Robert Schalkenbach Foundation, 1946 [first published in 1892].

"   *Progress and Poverty*. New York: The Robert Schalkenbach Foundation, 1960 [first published in 1879].

George, Henry, Jr. *The Life of Henry George*. New York: The Robert Schalkenbach Foundation, 1960 [first published in 1900].

Hirshleifer, Jack. "The Private and Social Value of Information and the Reward to Inventive Activity," *American Economic Review 62* (1972), pp. 561-74.

Hotelling, Harold. "The General Welfare in Relation to Problems of Taxation and of Railway and Utility Rates," *Econometrica 6* (1938), pp. 242-69.

Krueger, Anne. 'The Political Economy of the Rent-Seeking Society," *American Economic Review 64* (1974), pp. 291-

Mathis, Edward J. and Charles E. Zech. "An Empirical Test: The Economic Effects of Land Value Taxation," *Growth and Change 13* (1982), pp. 2-5.

Meek, Ronald L. *The Economics of Physiocracy*. Cambridge, MA: Harvard University Press, 1963.

McCulloch, John R. *A Treatise on the Principles and Practical Influence of Taxation and the Funding System*. New York: August M. Kelley, 1968 [reprint of the second edition of 1852].

Mieskowski, Peter and George R. Zodrow. "Taxation and the Tiebout Model," *Journal of Economic Literature 27* (1989), pp. 1098-1146.

Milgrom, Paul and Robert J. Weber. "A Theory of Auctions and Competitive Bidding," *Econometrica 50* (1982), pp. 1089-1122.

Mill, James. *Elements of Political Economy*. London: Baldwin Cradock and Joy, 1824.

Mill, John Stuart. *Collected Works*, Vol III., *Principles of Political Economy with Some of Their Applications to Social Philosophy*, Books III-V. Toronto: University of Toronto Press, 1965 [first published in 1848].

Mills, David E. "The Non-Neutrality of Land Taxation," *National Tax Journal 34* (1981), pp. 125-30.

"   "Reply to Tideman," *National Tax Journal 35* (1982), p. 115.

Nichols, Don. "Land and Economic Growth," *American Economic Review 60* (1970), pp. 332-40.

Noguchi, Yukio. "On the Intertemporal Non-Neutrality of Taxes on Land: A Dynamic Market Clearing Model," *Hitotsubashi Journal of Economics 22*

(1981), pp. 20-31.

Owen, Michael S. and Wayne Thirsk, "Land Taxes and Idle Land: A Case Study of Houston," *Land Economics 50* (1974), pp. 251-60.

Pillai, Vel. "Property Taxation in Thailand: An Uncommon Combination of a Land Tax and a Rental Tax," *Singapore Economic Review 32* (1987), pp. 43-53.

Post, Louis F. *The Prophet of San Francisco.* New York: The Robert Schalkenbach Foundation, 1930.

Prest, A. R. "Some Issues in Australian Land Taxation," *Environment and Planning C: Government and Policy 3* (1985), pp. 97-110.

Quesnay, François. "The 'General Maxims for the Economic Government of an Agricultural Kingdom,'" in Ronald L. Meek, 1963, pp. 231-62 [first published in 1756].

Rothbard, Murray. *The Ethics of Liberty.* Atlantic Highlands: Humanities Press, 1982.

Ricardo, David. *The Principles of Political Economy and Taxation.* New York: E. P. Dutton, 1911 [first published in 1817].

Samuelson, Paul A. "Intertemporal Price Equilibrium: A Prologue to the Theory of Speculation," *Weltwirtschaftliches Archiv 79* (1957), pp. 181-219, reprinted in *The Collected Scientific Papers of Paul A. Samuelson.* Ed.: Joseph E. Stiglitz. Cambridge, Mass.: MIT Press, 1966, Vol. 2, pp. 946-84.

Shoup, Donald C. "Advance Land Acquisition by Local Governments: A Cost-Benefit Analysis," *Yale Economic Essays 9* (1969), pp. 147-207.

"   "The Optimal Timing of Urban Development," *Papers of the Regional Science Association 25* (1970), pp. 33-44.

Skouras, Athanassios. "The Non-Neutrality of Land Taxation," *Public Finance 33* (1978), pp. 113-34.

Smith, Adam. *The Wealth of Nations.* New York: Random House, 1937 [first published in 1776].

Smolensky, Eugene, Richard Burton and Nicolaus Tideman. "The Efficient Provision of a Local Non-Private Good," *Geographical Analysis 2* (July 1970), pp. 330-42.

Stiglitz, J. E. "Public Goods in Open Economies with Heterogeneous Individuals," Oxford, mimeo, 1978.

Taussig, Frank. *Principles of Economics.* New York: Macmillan, 1916.

Thirsk, Wayne R. "The Capitalization of the Property Tax and Idle Land: Reply," *Land Economics 55* (1979), pp. 549-52.

Tideman, Nicolaus. "A Tax on Land *is* Neutral," *National Tax Journal 35* (1982), pp. 109-111.

"   "Takings, Moral Evolution and Justice," *Columbia Law Review 88* (1988), pp. 1714-30.

"   "Integrating Land-Value Taxation with the Internalization of Spatial Externalities," *Land Economics 66* (1990), pp. 341-55.

"   "Commons and Commonwealths: A New Framework for the Justification of Territorial Claims," in *Commons Without Tragedy*. Ed.: Robert Andelson. Savage, Maryland: Barnes and Noble (1991), pp. 109-29.

Turnbull, Geoffrey K. "The Effects of Local Taxes and Public Services on Residential Development," *Journal of Regional Science 28* (1988), pp. 541-62.

Vickrey, William. "The City as a Firm," in *The Economics of Public Services*. Eds.: Martin S. Feldstein and Robert P. Inman. Hampshire: Macmillan, 1977, pp. 334-43.

Wildasin, David E. "More on the Neutrality of Land Taxes," *National Tax Journal 35* (1982), pp. 105-08.

Poverty and the Theory of Wages: a "Geoclassical" analysis
Fred E. Foldvary

The marginal revolution in economic theory not only introduced the concept of marginal utility but also homogenized land and capital goods to the point where the important distinction between them was blurred. Simple neoclassical models use a two-factor model, with capital and labor, contrary to the classical models's primary use of land and labor. Labor demand curves are derived top-down from fiat macro production functions. The mathematical treatment of the marginal productivity of factors masks an asymmetry in the economic nature of land and labor, and leaves the neoclassical paradigm without any deep explanation of the wage level. In the spirit of Joseph Schumpeter's work, this chapter is an analysis of the historical thought on wage theory. I conclude that Henry George's theory of wage determination, which based the marginal product of labor at zero-rent marginal land, provides a link between classical and neoclassical theory that deepens the theory of the determination of wage levels and offers the only coherent theory of poverty in modern industrial society.

In analyzing the theory of the determination of the wage level, some key terms will first be defined. Using the meaning provided by Henry George (1879, p. 32), "the term labor includes all human exertion in the production of wealth, and wages, being that part of the produce which goes to labor, includes all reward for such exertion." As recognized also by Carl Menger (1871, p. 172), "*Entrepreneurial activity* must definitely be counted as a category of labor services." Hence in the taxonomy of returns to factors, entrepreneurial profits constitute wages as well.

The "wage level" is defined here, to give it some measurable meaning, as an index of the median annual market wage of unskilled workers within some territory in which there is a free movement of labor. Paul Douglas (1934, p. 16) defended the abstraction of minimally skilled labor as having empirical usage: "In common practice business men deal with such units of labor when they contract for the average run of unskilled labor, and the rate for this class furnishes in turn the basing point upon which the differentials for the other classes of labor are erected."

Wages of better skilled or talented workers are based on the wage level, having a premium as a return on human capital, charm, talent, effort, personal connections, scarcity, disutility, legal-restriction rents, discrimination, and other factors. Ludwig von Mises (1949, p. 606) noted that the "institutional fixing of wage rates is one of the most important features of our age of interventionist policies." Hence, the analysis here concerns the wage level prevailing in an unhampered market.

A theory of the determination of some wage level distinguishes between the wage level at some moment in time, relative to returns to other factors, and the evolution of the wage level during some time interval. Another distinction is the relative wage level, the proportion of output going to wages, and the absolute wage level, the amount of goods that can be exchanged for an hour of labor.

The existence of an absolute wage level becomes apparent when one compares the wages of labor in less-developed countries (LDCs) and more-developed countries (MDCs). For example, barbers, though possessing similar capital goods and skill, are commonly observed to earn greater purchasing power in MDCs than in LDCs.

The Austrian theory of wages

A theory of wages logically begins with the Austrian theory of higher-order (non-consumer) goods or factors. In contrast to the labor theory of value attributing goods value from labor value, Carl Menger (1871) recognized that goods have a subjective value. He then deduced that the value of goods of higher order derived from that of the goods of lower order that they help produce. In particular, the price of labor services is governed "by the magnitude of importance of the satisfactions that would have to remain unsatisfied if we were unable to command labor services" (p. 171). As Ludwig von Mises (1949, p. 271) recognized, wages are ultimately paid not by employers but by consumers. This is consistent with and enriches classical theory; at the zero-rent margin of production, abstracting from capital goods, the wage consists of the product and the wage level is equal to the product's subjective value.

But by itself, Austrian theory does not explain where along the diminishing marginal utility of the product and hence of labor the wage level is set. Labor will be exerted until the marginal utility of its product equals that of leisure, but an explanation for the return to labor relative to that of land and capital goods is not fully provided by marginal productivity alone.

Neoclassical wage determination
The neoclassical paradigm of economics lacks a full and deep explanation for the level of wages in an economy. Microeconomic theory assumes the existence of some wage and explains the number of workers hired by a firm as set where the value of the marginal product of labor equals the wage. Turgot (1768) and later Malthus (1915) and West (1815) had recognized the law of variable proportions or diminishing returns for combined labor and capital. But even when labor is separated from capital, as done by Von Thünen (1842), this law does not account for the wage level, since it by itself does not determine the point along the diminishing increments where the wage rate will be set. The wage level in some economy such as a country exists in the domain of macroeconomics.

The neoclassical revolution in economics that took place during the latter part of the 19th century begat a macroeconomic paradigm which split into several factions. However, there is no explanation of how the wage level that does prevail came to be. The "new-classical" school, which arose in the 1970s as an expression of dissatisfaction with Keynesianism, does have a theory of wage determination, but it is incomplete. The labor market has an aggregate demand curve and some upward-sloping supply curve, perhaps backward sloping at some high wage, and the intersection is the wage that prevails if there is no intervention into the market process. In the Keynesian school, the nominal wage is either exogenous or else essentially uses the neoclassical model, but with a time lag, so that wages can remain stuck or sticky at some level when the supply and demand curves shift to lower the intersection between demand and supply.

Even the "new classical" macro labor-market model begs the question. Neoclassical theory only states that there will be some market-determined wage level, but not what that level is, or how it is determined. The wage level depends on the shape and location of the aggregate labor supply and demand curves. The theory does partly explain the labor demand curve. There is some aggregate production function, with output as a function of labor. The function has a positive first derivative and, due to diminishing returns when labor is variable and other factors fixed, a negative second derivative. Hence, each additional worker has a positive marginal product, but less than the previous worker.

The demand for a marginal worker is this marginal product, hence the downward-sloping demand curve in accord with the law of demand. However, the location and slope of demand for given numbers of workers, which explains how the marginal product of labor is set, is left without a deep explanation. Alfred Marshall (1920, p. 518) recognized this: "The doctrine that the earnings of a worker tend to be equal to the net product of his work, has by itself no real meaning," although "the doctrine throws into clear light the action of one of the causes that govern wages."

Paul Douglas (1948, p. 5) notes that theorists have had "little interest in trying to determine ... the positions and slopes of these curves." He himself engaged in empirical research on the contributions to production by labor and capital, using the Cobb-Douglas production function, and found that during 1899-1922, the U.S. labor exponent was about 0.63, hence the marginal wage is 63% of total marginal product. Such research could test a theory of wage determination, but by itself it does not provide any explanation of how the wage level is set, e.g. why the figure is 0.63 and not something else, and why that figure stays constant.

The key determinant of the real-wage level is the location at which the labor supply curve cuts the demand curve. If the aggregate production function is assumed to be linearly homogenous, then by Euler's theorem, total output equals the sum of the marginal products of each factor times the quantity of the respective factors. This relationship, pioneered by Philip Wicksteed (1894), provides a mathematically convenient premise used, for example, in the macroeconomic model by Thomas Sargent (1979).Given two factors labor and capital, the marginal product of labor is fixed at any moment, determined by the ratio of labor to capital and the change in output as the ratio changes, symmetric with the marginal product of capital.

Though useful for purposes of macro modelling and for the theory of atomistic competition, a linearly homogenous two-factor production function omits the macroeconomic effects of land, which can in practice be different from those of capital. The model assumes that all capital is homogenous, which is not realistic for land. Interestingly, it achieves its results by treating capital like expandable land, its marginal product being a residual: capital at any moment is fixed, and given that (i) the sum of the exponents is *1*, and (ii) some exponent *a* for labor, the exponent for capital must be the residual *1 - a*, like a land rent.

Macroeconomic texts typically posit that the labor supply curve is an increasing function of the real wage. Michael Parkin (1984, p. 114), for example, states, "The theory of household behavior predicts that utility-maximizing households will supply more hours of labor as the real wage increases up to some maximum." But the premise is arbitrary. Its justification is that a higher bid is required in order to shift a worker from one job to another. But suppose the worker is unemployed. Then no higher bid may be needed relative to the bid for the previous worker. It is also possible for several workers to shift at the next wage increment. So long as some workers are unemployed, the supply could be partly horizontal. Indeed, in classical theory, the supply curve of labor is just that.

Ricardian-classical wage theory
Classical theory has two explanations of wage determination, the wages fund and subsistence. According to Joseph Schumpeter (1954, p. 268), Adam Smith presented "the first fully systematic treatment of" labor economics. Smith (1776, Vol. I, p. 76) stated that "there is ... a certain rate below which it seems impossible to reduce ... ordinary wages," namely that level necessary to maintain a worker and his family. Smith cites Cantillon (1775) as proposing that family subsistence is at least double that of the adult worker. As Schumpeter (1954, p. 663) notes, such minimum-of-existence propositions, which had been proposed earlier by Quesnay and Turgot, do not constitute a theory of wages but a theorem about the long-run equilibrium level of wages.

Smith (1776) recognized that wages can be above subsistence if there is sufficient demand relative to supply, made effective by "funds which are destined for the payment of wages" (p. 77), the wages fund. An increase in national wealth leads to an increase in the demand for and wages of labor (p. 78). When growth ceases, even if per-capita wealth is high, wages will not be so high, since the supply of labor will have increased (p. 79). But Smith does not provide a more specific explanation of how the wage level is set when it is above subsistence. Schumpeter (1954, p. 268) wrote that Smith's exposition foreshadowed subsequent theories of labor exploitation and bargaining power. These theories, which posit that price competition drives down wages unless protected by unions and legislation, have predominated in labor economics, as noted by Douglas (1948).

In David Ricardo's (1821) model, the "natural price of labour is that price which is necessary to enable the labourers, one with another, to subsist" due to the Malthusian expansion of the labor force until the diminishing marginal product of labor hits that minimum level. Hence the wage level is horizontal until all households have employment. The model can be generalized in the following way. Suppose there are identical households, each with two adults. Children are not part of the labor force. All households have insufficient savings to allow subsistence for more than a very short time. The subjective value of leisure differs among the individuals, but for all persons, leisure has a positive value, and survival is preferred to non-survival. There is some subsistence wage that enables one person to obtain the bare necessities of life for a family. Absolute poverty is defined as a household income at the subsistence wage or below. There are no interventions (i.e. taxes, restrictions, unemployment compensation or welfare assistance) on labor and enterprise.

The labor supply curve will be horizontal at the subsistence level, up to n workers, since one adult from each household will accept that wage rather than perish. When all households are employed, then the supply curve becomes upward sloping. Adults with the lowest opportunity cost of working are hired, and with increasing opportunity costs, ever higher wages are required to compensate the second adult in a household for the lost leisure. Once all adults have employment, the labor supply curve is vertical. One could extend the model to have a backward sloping curve above some wage level, but that is not a relevant issue here.

This model explains both poverty and chronic unemployment even with an unrestricted market (e.g. without minimum-wage laws). If the labor demand curve crosses the supply curve in its horizontal section, then not only are all workers poor, but the labor supply between the supply/demand intersection point and the employment of all households is unemployed, since these workers would be willing to work at the same wage. The neoclassical concept of "full" employment becomes ambiguous, since the unemployment can be long term and is non-cyclical and non-structural.

The Ricardian employment model may be in accord with the labor market in many less-developed countries but it fails to account for the wage level in more-developed economies such as in Australia, Japan, North America and Western Europe, where much of even unskilled labor is able to obtain an income greater than mere subsistence. (The existence of the homeless and unemployed in MDCs who do live close to subsistence cannot necessarily be explained by the Ricardian model, since these might be explained by the substandard quality of the labor as well as by interventions such as laws mandating above-subsistence wages and housing quality.) The Ricardian model's premise of a subsistence wage does not hold if technological and organizational improvements increase productivity at a greater rate than population growth. And as Schumpeter (1954, p. 664) wrote, "The element of productivity theory" was "not adequately worked out" in classical thought. Schumpeter (p. 665) also noted that if the minimum of existence is interpreted as a socially-acceptable minimum, then it becomes "an institutional datum," an exogenous, unexplained variable.

Henry George's wage theory
A model that does explain the process by which both poverty and super-subsistence wage levels are determined is that presented by Henry George in *Progress and Poverty* (1879). In George's theory, the wage level is not presumed, but is a phenomenon to be explained. First, George (p. 23) rejects the classical wages-fund theory, arguing "That wages, instead of being drawn from capital, are in reality drawn from the product of the labor for which they are paid." To George, the refutation of the wage-fund fallacy also implied the rejection of dependent notions such as "the vulgar theories ... that the sum to be distributed in wages is a fixed one," so that wages decrease as the labor force increases (p. 25).

In explaining this marginal product, George's methodology is to begin with a simple model that elucidates the main principles: "society in its most highly developed form is but an elaboration of society in its rudest beginnings" (1879, p. 27). Complexities are added subsequently, one at a time.

The model first abstracts from capital goods; as with previous classical theory, the two original factors of production are land and labor. Workers are identical, there is one worker per household, and there is only one product, corn. The land is divided into areas with differing fertility.

George sets in motion a dynamic scenario which begins with an unpopulated territory. Immigrants arrive one at a time, and there is some uniform size of land that a settler may claim; implicitly, this is the area that a worker can cultivate in some normal work day, and each farm has an identical amount of labor applied to it. George analyzes the effect on wages and land rent. His main premise is the maximizing principle: workers will attempt to maximize their income for any given resource constraint. The first settlers claim the most fertile land. Since land is free, rent is zero, and the entire amount of the product constitutes wages.

Asymmetrical land and labor
We can see here a foundational distinction between land and labor made by classical theory. The key question is: why does the product constitute wages and not rent? The obvious answer, provided by George, is that land is free. But suppose there were an unlimited number of workers available. Why would labor also not be free, or paid such a pittance as to be practically free?

To probe into this question, suppose the workers were not human beings but androids, robots who functioned as human beings, and there were an unlimited supply available at no cost (just as land has no cost of production). Suppose also that the land was divided into plots, each of which had a living, conscious, sentient mind. When the first worker came to the best-quality land, the corn would be claimed by the land-being, not the worker-robot, even though the land-being was passive while the robot did the work. Thus, the entire product would constitute land rent, not wages. In George's model, the product is ascribed to wages because labor is the sentient agent. The product goes to the sentient factor: "the human element is the initiative or active factor - that which begins or acts first. The natural element is the passive factor - that which receives action and responds to it" (George, 1897, p. 77). This asymmetry was recognized at least as far back as Sir William Petty (1662), who referred to labor as the "active principle of wealth."

This asymmetric distinction between land and labor has been all but lost in the neoclassical paradigm. In mathematical treatments of marginal productivity, all factors are treated as algebraicly symmetric. Moreover, aside from minor mention in passing in principles texts, land as a factor of production has been largely folded into capital goods. Both the homogenization of factors and the elimination of land as a major factor preclude a determination of the wage level. If labor is symmetric with capital, differing only in being more variable in the short run, then wages can only be determined relative to the productivity and amount of capital, but capital is created by and uses labor, so this mutual dependency leaves the wage level undetermined unless there is some production function set by fiat, leaving the marginal product of capital goods as a residual. By eliminating land, the neoclassical revolution threw the baby out with the bath water.

The geoclassical theory of wages
The Georgist model provides a foundation for the wage level in its asymmetric treatment of the original factors, land and labor. George's theory is neither purely classical nor neoclassical. "George challenged, modified, and in some instances eliminated the clusters of theories and auxiliary propositions lying within the orbit of the classical protective belt" (Petrella, 1988, p. 381). It can be termed "geoclassical" as both Georgist and land-based. Since land has no cost of production and is not sentient, where land of a given quality is free for the taking, output is ascribed to wages. This is Henry George's "law of wages": *wages are determined by productivity at the extensive margin of production*. This extensive margin of production consists of the most productive land available at no marginal cost. The production function is grounded on the productivity of land and labor. The asymmetric treatment of land enables there to be a foundation upon which the wage structure is based: the margin where land rent is zero.

In the corn model, the margin of cultivation is the best free land that an immigrant farmer would claim. Let us set the subsistence wage at two and assign to land integers standing for the productivity of a plot, ranging from zero to ten. If the margin is at land yielding ten, then wages are ten, substantially above subsistence. Hence, with George, there is no inevitable iron law of wages that necessarily destines labor to subsistence. Wages depend on the productivity of the margin, whatever it happens to be. However, George does note the prevalence of subsistence wages throughout the world, and his theory attempts to explain why with certain institutional settings, namely those prevailing in the economies of his time (and still today), there is a "tendency ... of wages to a minimum" (p. 17), despite the great increase in global wealth and technology. Hence the title of his work.

To continue the dynamic model, when all the best land, e.g. yielding ten, is claimed, then subsequent immigrants claim the next best land. The margin moves from a yield of ten to that of nine. Wages at the margin are nine, and since workers are identical, competition makes wages at the ten-land also nine. The ten-land now has a rent of one. George thus formulates his "law of rent": rent is the difference between the yield of land and that land at the margin of production, given the same quality of labor. A complication that neither George nor Ricardo considered is that since land of higher productivity will also have an intensive margin, with more workers per plot than less-productive land, the total quantity of labor will be higher on more productive land. But since the extra labor further increases the product and the rent of the better land, taking into account the intensive margin makes the relative increase in rent even greater. The wage level is still set at the extensive margin where land is free.

As immigrants continue to arrive, each grade of land becomes fully claimed and the margin moves stepwise to land yielding ever less until the margin reaches the subsistence level. At that point, all wages are now at subsistence, the remainder of the product of lands better than the margin being a rental yield going to the owners of the land plots. Hence, with population growth, wages can eventually reach the subsistence level. This subsistence level has not been assumed, but is a consequence of population, the quality of land, and labor productivity. Note, however, that while, other things equal, increased population by itself will move the margin towards less productive land, George also held that other things are not equal, since increased population may have increasing organizational returns, and also that production could move towards lower margins even without population growth.

Whereas Smith (1776, Vol. I, p. 78) held that progress raises wages, George argued that wages could fall not despite of but even because of progress: *"with increase in productive power, rent tends to even greater increase, thus producing a constant tendency to the forcing down of wages"* (1879, p. 282, emphasis in original). This can happen due to "invention and improvement" even "though population should remain stationary" (p. 251). Although increasing productivity may at first raise wages, if the margin of production moves towards less productive land, wages again fall, the increase in wealth going to land rent instead. When the economy is expanding, because of the fixed (or at least highly inelastic) supply of land, people realize that land rent and values are rising, and will therefore obtain land for speculation as well as use. Some of this speculative land will not be put to its full economic present-day use, since it may be more profitable to sell and build later. This moves the margin of production out faster than it would without speculation, further depressing wages and increasing rent.

Do rent-free margins exist?

Critics of the concept of a zero-rent margin argue that nowadays all land has a positive rent, the rent of the poorest land in use being determined by its positive marginal product. But even today, there are large areas of desert and mountain which have no economic activity. There is also a margin at the oceans, being economic land where fishing provides for wages as well as rents. The "margin" most broadly involves successively relative margins, sites at the border of any particular usage, such as the edge of a city for urban uses, e.g. where urban land prices depend on agricultural land prices, which in turn depend on a no-rent margin. Also, even when all surface land has a positive rent, a rent-free extensive margin still exists, since the urban margin includes the air space above buildings. An additional story may be built with no increase in the site rent for that plot of land.

Suppose, though, that an isolated island contains land of uniform quality which is entirely settled, and that the owners of land are distinct from the laborers. Abstracting from capital goods, the margin is the ocean, where by premise the product of labor is zero (ruling out fishing). So long as land is available for free, the entire product goes to wages, but as soon as all land is taken, the extensive marginal product of labor falls to zero, and landowners can extract all the rent above the minimum that workers require to live on. The entire product minus the subsistence wage goes to rent. However, once all households are employed at subsistence, the labor supply curve becomes an increasing function of wages (for a second adult in each household), and the wage will be higher than subsistence so long as the marginal cost of labor is not greater than the marginal product. Hence, the wage level would be set where the marginal labor cost equals the marginal goods product, with the remainder of the product going to rent. But the very reason that the remainder goes to rent and not wages is still the existence of the extensive margin at the ocean, enabling land owners to obtain this rent. Note also that if the number of households then increases, the horizontal section of the supply curve is pushed out, lowering the wage until, ultimately, it again reaches subsistence.

Hence, even when all available solid-surface land has a rent, the extensive land margin is still ultimately a factor in determining the rent due to the fixed supply of land of a given quality, for if the supply were infinite, rent would be zero.

Complications added to the model to make it more complete do not change its essential principles. Adding capital goods increases the product at the margin and splits the product between wages and a return to capital goods. The net effect is to increase wages as well as rent, equalizing total returns to the production of consumer and capital goods, discounted by the real interest rate during production. John Bates Clark (1902) theorized that there could also be a marginal zone for capital goods in antiquated machinery with no capital yields (Douglas, 1934, p. 62). However, such zones would be less universal than that of land.

Better technology also increases the yield at the margin of production, hence increases wages as well as rent. So with productive technology and with ever more capital goods, production at the margin need not be at subsistence. However, notes George, such technology can make previously submarginal land more productive, which can move the margin again to less productive land, lowering wages once again. Finally, the one-crop model can be generalized to several crops and to non-agricultural production.

If land of super-subsistence yield is available for free, wages will be above subsistence, and there is with George no law dictating that the population must necessarily rise until the margin reaches subsistence. Moreover, George goes to great lengths to argue against the Malthusian proposition that population growth will tend to outrace agricultural production. George argues that the movement of labor to less productive land can be offset by the greater productivity that a greater division of labor can bring about, aside from technological improvements and added capital. We thus have a theory explaining the wage level of both LDCs and MDCs, where technology, organization, division of labor, and the quality of both land and labor determine the productivity of labor at a zero-rent margin of production, hence the wage level. Land rent is the residual yield of super-marginal land after subtracting wages and capital yields from the total product.

The policy implication of this theory is that conventional fiscal and regulatory policy place economies inside their production possibility curves. Both output and wages can be increased by eliminating the taxation and arbitrary restriction of labor and enterprise and instead tapping economic land rents for public revenue. "To abolish the taxation which, acting and reacting, now hampers every wheel of exchange and presses upon every form of industry, would be like removing an immense weight from a powerful spring" (George, 1879, p. 434). George's second reason why the community collection of rent would increase wages is that it induces a more efficient use of land, moving the margin towards higher productivity and therefore higher wages.

A geoclassical macroeconomic model
George's theory goes beyond wage determination to form a paradigm of macroeconomics substantially different from both classical and neoclassical models. This paradigm was not explicitly set forth by George, but it can be derived from his basic principles, synthesized with Austrian and neoclassical concepts, hence termed here "geoclassical" rather than Georgist. Whereas in the neoclassical paradigm, the wage is derived from a fiat aggregate production function, in this synthesis, the production function is endogenous, computed by the model. This corresponds to how the GDP is computed empirically; realistically, deriving the wage level from a fiat aggregate production function puts the cart before the horse.

In the geoclassical macro model, exogenous variables include land, a stock of antique capital goods, technology at some moment, an interest rate determined by time preference, and a labor supply curve. There is one consumer good, and labor has a uniform quality. There are two capital goods, the antique good and the good producible with current technology. The land has a fixed area and is divided into several zones differing in productivity; within each zone, there is a given intensive marginal labor productivity. Each firm uses an identical area of land in each zone. The model is generated dynamically, letting the labor force grow from zero so long as with that labor force, the marginal product of labor is not less than the wage a worker is willing to receive.

The first workers use land with the highest productivity. Antique capital goods are available free; new capital goods can be created from the given technology, using labor, antique capital goods, and land. With the given technology, a unit of new capital goods increases production by a given percentage and requires a given duration of labor to produce, while the producer borrows the consumer good at the wage level with antique goods during that interval. A unit of land is also required, which at first is free.

The amount of capital produced will thus be a function of its marginal yield, time, and the interest rate, such that wages earned from producing capital goods will be equal to those producing the consumer good. With that amount of new capital goods, the total production for each firm is determined, hence also the production function for the zone. After the best zone is used up, its total production is the sum of the production of the firms.

The margin of production moves to the next best land. The production at that zone is determined the same way. Now, land at the best zone has acquired a rent, and the lower wage level makes it possible for additional workers to be hired and more capital produced there until their intensive marginal products equal that at the extensive margin. The total product is now the sum of the product of the two zones, and the production function is composed of the sum of those of the zones, with the marginal products of labor and capital goods equalized, but that of land differing.

Production then moves to zones of successively less productivity until the extensive marginal product of labor is less than that which the labor supply is willing to provide. The model can then be made more complex. If the agents are able to claim land that is not immediately put to use, land speculation will occur, swiftly moving the margin out, lowering wages and raising rent by substantially more than without speculation. If the rent is collected and distributed equally to all the parties, such speculation is avoided, and incomes become equalized, since wages are equal and interest compensates for postponing consumption. The model can also be expanded with several goods, different qualities of labor, heterogenous capital goods with several levels of roundaboutness, and so on. Such complications would not change the basic principle of wage determination at the zero-rent margin.

The geoclassical synthesis
Henry George's theory of wage determination provides a foundation upon which neoclassical and Austrian analysis can be integrated to create a more complete theory, with the production function a result rather than a parameter of the model. Austrian theory explains wages as ultimately determined by the subjective valuations of consumer goods. George's theory explains the wage level relative to rent and relative to the amount of goods obtainable as based on productivity at extensive zero-rent margins. Neoclassical theory is applied to determine the quantity of labor at intensive margins. The synthesis can potentially explain the evolution of capital goods and wages as a function of diminishing returns on extensive land margins, the amount of and productivity of capital goods, increasing returns on technology and the division of labor, and returns based on the ratio of labor both to land and to capital. The wage level has institutional dependencies, affected especially by fiscal and regulatory policy, wages being increased when public revenues tap land rather than labor.

References

Cantillon, Richard (1775), *Essai sur la Nature du Commerce en général.*
Clark, John Bates (1902), *The Distribution of Wealth: A Theory of Wages, Interest and Profits.* New York and London: Macmillan Co.
Douglas, Paul H. 1948 [1964]. "Are There Laws of Production?" *American Economic Review* 38, 1 (March). In Douglas (1934 [1964]): 1-41.
——————. 1934 (1964), *The Theory of Wages.* New York: Augustus M. Kelly.

George, Henry, 1879 [1975], *Progress and Poverty*. New York: Robert Schalkenbach Foundation.

—————, 1897 [1968], *The Science of Political Economy*. New York: Robert Schalkenbach Foundation.

Malthus, Thomas (1815), *Nature and Progress of Rent*.

Marshall, Alfred, 1920 [1961], *Principles of Economics*. London: Macmillan and Company.

Menger, Carl, 1871 [1976]. *Principles of Economics*. Trans. James Dingwall and Bert Hoselitz. New York: New York University Press.

Mises, Ludwig von, 1949 [1966]. *Human Action*. New Haven: Yale University Press, and Henry Regnery Company.

Parkin, Michael (1984), *Macroeconomics*. Englewood Cliffs: Prentice-Hall.

Petrella, Frank (1988). "Henry George and the Classical Scientific Research Program: George's Modification of It and His Real Significance for Future Generations." *American Journal of Economics and Sociology* 47, no. 3 (July): 371-384.

Petty, Sir William (1662), *A Treatise of Taxes and Contributions*.

Ricardo, David, 1821 [1911], *The Principles of Political Economy and Taxation*. Third edition. London: Dent.

Sargent, Thomas (1979), *Macroeconomic Theory*. New York: Academic Press.

Schumpeter, Joseph A., 1954 [1986], *History of Economic Analysis* (Ed. Elizabeth Schumpeter). New York: Oxford University Press.

Smith, Adam, 1776 [1976], *The Wealth of Nations*, 2 volumes (Ed. Edwin Canaan). Chicago: University of Chicago Press.

Thünen, Johann Heinrich von, 1842 [1930], *Der Isolierte Staat*. Rpt. G. Fischer Jena, 1930.

Turgot, Anne-Robert Jacques, 1768 (1844), Oeuvres.

West, Edward (1815), *The Application of Capital to Land*.

Wicksteed, Philip (1894), *An Essay on the Coördination of the Laws of Distribution*, London: Macmillan & Co.

Flawed Land Acts 1947-1976

V. H. Blundell

Since 1945, many attempts have been made in Britain by both Labour and Conservative governments to pass legislation which would have direct or indirect bearing on land economics. Most of that legislation, from Labour's Town and Country Planning Act of 1947 down to the Conservative introduction of the Community Charge in the late 1980s, has produced very important side-effects which were obviously not anticipated or intended by Parliament. These side-effects arose through a failure properly to appreciate certain fundamental economic principles, including the very meaning of the word "land".

Land reformers of various kinds have long contended that the adverse effects of the land tenure system prevailing in England and Wales, and also (with some important variations) in Scotland, lead directly and indirectly to a wide range of social and economic problems. Among these are high costs of housing, homelessness, unemployment, high taxation and recurrent industrial depressions. The present essay is primarily concerned with those particular aspects of the "land question", although some reference will be made to other aspects as well.

In the early part of the 20th Century, agitation for land reform became a major political issue. In 1903, the Conservatives enacted some important land legislation relating to Ireland, whose effects, good and bad, are visible in both the north and the south to this day. A few years later, their Liberal successors attempted to assess land values in Scotland as a preliminary to taxation, but were frustrated by the House of Lords. The land taxing clauses of Lloyd George's 1909 Budget inaugurated one of the most intense periods of political controversy in modern history. There was continuing interest in land reform in the inter-war years: substantial legal reforms achieved by the Conservative government in 1925; the derating of agricultural land in 1929; the effort of the Labour Government in 1931 to assess and tax land values; and the unsuccessful London Rating (Site Value) Bill of 1938.

We are concerned with legislative measures which have been made, or attempted, since 1945. We will not consider all legislation which has some bearing on land - that would be an almost impossible task - but only the legislation which was primarily concerned to secure for the community some of those land values which were created by the community, but in practice were captured by private individuals. It is the view of the author that in many - perhaps most - of these cases Parliament was motivated by thoroughly creditable principles, but that the effects actually produced were widely different from those intended, and sometimes the very reverse, through a misunderstanding of the underlying economics. If Britain is about to undergo a further spate of land legislation in the near future, it is important that the strengths and weaknesses of past measures should be clearly understood, in order that avoidable errors should not be repeated.

Definition
The word "land" will be used repeatedly. The term is here usually employed in its economic sense, to cover all natural resources. In actual pieces of legislation, however, the word is used in its legal sense, which includes buildings and other developments set upon land. These two usages of the same word must perforce be followed, but it is important that the reader should appreciate the ambiguity.

The Town and Country Planning Act, 1947
The background
In the first half of the 20th Century, both the Labour and Liberal Parties were more or less formally committed to land value taxation. A considerable number of Conservatives, including Winston Churchill, showed much sympathy with the idea as well. When the Labour Party came to power in 1945, it was eagerly expected by many of its supporters, and by land reformers generally, that land value taxation would be introduced.

The Town and Country Planning Act which was passed in 1947 is famous for a number of its provisions. It greatly strengthened the control of local authorities over planning and land use. These element of the Act are extremely important, but they lie rather outside the present study. The provisions which are most relevant here are those which concerned "betterment" values.

The Act brought together the recommendations of the Scott, Barlow and Uthwatt Reports, which drew attention to the high cost to local authorities and government corporations of acquiring land for development. These Reports noted that, as soon as development was mooted, a "cloud" of value descended on the designated area, and up went the price of land. This "cloud" of land speculation followed the planners around the country.

If planning decisions by public authorities gave rise to increased land values, it was argued, then the "betterment" of land value should pass to the community, and not to the landowners. Hence a "betterment" charge should be levied. All increases in land values which were not related to planning permission, however, were to be excluded from this charge. The architects of the Act claimed that it would end land speculation, force land into use, and ensure that increased land values arising from the release of land for development accrued to the community.

Provisions of the Act

The basic provisions of the Act which are relevant here were as follows:

a. The right to develop land became a state monopoly, and permission to develop, or change the use of, land had to be bought from the newly-created Central Land Board. The definition of "development" was therefore not confined to construction on vacant sites and the re-development of existing buildings. It also included the change of use of buildings from one business to another.

b. When "development", within the special meaning of the Act, required planning permission, it attracted a Development Charge. The Act, however, laid down twenty-two classes of undertakings or occupations which were to be considered as of a similar nature. A change of use within a class was not deemed to involve "development", and was therefore exempt from Development Charge. But a change of use from one class to another required planning permission and, if granted, attracted a Development Charge. As an example, shops as such were not a single class of use. The class into which a shop was placed depended on what it sold. A person could not change from selling sweets to selling tripe, or vice versa, without planning permission - which, if granted, made him liable to a Development Charge.

c. The method of calculating the amount of Development Charge payable was to take the assumed selling value of a property if it was confined to its present use - "existing use value", as this was called - and deduct this from the value of the property with permission for its development potential to be realised. The difference between the two values was taxed at 100 per cent.

d. A sum of £300 millions was made available as compensation to land owners who could claim hardship because their land was ripe for development, but the Central Land Board had refused them the right to develop.

The Act was passed in August 1947, and the planning sections took effect shortly afterwards. The rest of the Act, which included the Development Charge (s.61) came into effect in July 1948.

Weaknesses of the Act

Although the Act was clearly an attempt to capture land values for the people, it had many practical defects. Anomalies and absurdities abounded, and even before the legislation came into operation many people in the professions concerned with development and use of land and buildings were alarmed at the complexity of rules, regulations and Orders. Mr Silkin, Minister of Town and Country Planning, admitted in a debate in the Commons (26 May 1948) to having second "or even third" thoughts on this "highly intricate matter". So complex was the Act that civil servants were sent round the country to address meetings on the workings of the Act for the benefit of those in local government and the professions who had to interpret, advise on, or administer the regulations.

But there were other defects of a more fundamental character. In the first place, the development charge which was intended to deprive the landowner of communally-created increases in land values fell only when the land was developed or redeveloped. Increases in land values arising from other causes remained with the landowners. In practice the vast majority of land value increases was of this kind, and these were therefore lost to the community.

In the second place, development was discouraged, since there was more profit to be made by improving property up to the limit of a change or use than improving or building beyond that level, when it would attract a Development Charge. The same applied to empty sites, which were used as car parks or for similar purposes. Idle land as such attracted no charge, and so site owners were encouraged to keep it idle, in the hope that - with a change of government - the financial provisions of the Act would be repealed.

A third weakness was that the Development Charge applied to the developed site as a "property", and not to the land itself. The greater the development the greater the charge, irrespective of the value of the land as a separate factor. This weakness seems to have derived from a fundamental misunderstanding of the nature of land values. These are determined not by the actual use to which a piece of land is put, but by its potential use in the mind of a prospective purchaser. People will often pay a great deal of money for piece of land which is more or less derelict, because they think that they can use it in a way which will bring them profit.

Finally, landowners who had been refused the right to develop their land - whether or not they were entitled to a share in the £300 millions compensation - were disposed to withhold it from sale, in the speculative hope that it would increase in value without, of course, attracting the Development Charge. Thus land speculation, so far from being ended, was actually encouraged.

Operation of the Act

As the Act came to be applied, a chorus of criticism and condemnation arose. Some, but by no means all, of this criticism was politically inspired. The Act was simply not working as the legislators had intended. There were examples from all over the country of frustration resulting from extortionate Development Charges, inconsistent rulings and valuations, absurd decisions, and differing interpretations of the regulations.

The Press reported numerous examples of the effects which the regulations were having on would-be developers, on those whose use changed from one class to another, and on those who innocently thought that they did not come within the scope of the regulations. One typical example was of a factory owner who was discouraged by the Development Charge from building on land that adjoined his factory. Instead, he erected two goal posts on the land, for his workers to play football. This was deemed a development, and charges were imposed on the goal posts. Another was of a man who bought his disused air raid shelter from the local Council. He was refused permission to use it as a tool shed unless he paid a Development Charge.

Many owners of small building plots who had previously bought them to build a house, faced a Development Charge which doubled the price they had paid for the land - the existing use value of which was deemed by the Central Land Board to be purely nominal. Valuers had no firm criteria for arriving at development values. They depended on the estimated value of the completed buildings, less the "existing use" - a vague and indeterminate concept. Many valuers had to back-track on their estimates when challenged on appeal.

Valuations under the Act were subjective and often perverse because of the underlying fallacy that the value of a plot is determined by what it is used for, or what is put upon it. Thus, two plots of land which on the market would fetch the same price had, by this reasoning, different values when used for different purposes.

At the root of these various defects was the fact that "land" was considered in its legal meaning, which included buildings and other improvements, and not in its economic sense, as natural resources alone. Thus the Development Charge was aptly named: it was a tax on development and use of land, not on the land itself.

But what of the claims that the Act would cheapen land, make it more readily available, and end speculation? Many landowners refused to part with their land, even under threats of compulsory purchase. They sat tight, waiting for amending legislation, or a change of government. They had nothing to lose, as compensation for loss of development rights was indeterminate and they were not interested in parting with their land at present-use value. Estate Agents reported that the supply of building land for sale had declined, and that when land was available its price was usually well in excess of current-use value.

Partial repeal of the Act

A Conservative government took office in 1951, and in December 1952 the financial provisions of the Town and Country Planning Act were repealed.

This ended the Development Charge, and also the obligation of the Government to distribute compensation to landowners.

Another provision of the Town and Country Planning Act, which has not been discussed above, had given public authorities the power to acquire land compulsorily in certain circumstances. This was no new principle in English law, and had many precedents in - for example - the Canal and Railway Acts. In some cases, land had been acquired under the Town and Country Planning Act 1947 at less than its market value. This state of affairs was also altered by Conservative legislation. A new Town and Country Planning Act was passed in 1959, which entitled the landowner whose land was compulsorily acquired to receive the market value, including any increases in market value arising from development plans.

The Land Commission
In 1964 the Labour Party returned to power, and in 1966 it received an increased majority. This gave it the opportunity to legislate once again for the recovery of betterment values, and to extend the powers of compulsory purchase of land.

Principles
There was no attempt to restore in their original form those clauses of the Town and Country Planning Act 1947 which the Conservatives had repealed, but an important new measure, the Land Commission Act, was passed in 1967. Its aims were said to be "to secure that the right land is available at the right time for the implementation of national, regional and local plans", and "to secure that a substantial part of the development value created by the community is returned to the community and that the burden of the cost of land for essential purposes is reduced".

The Land Commission Act, 1967
To achieve these objectives, several legislative changes were made. The Act was long and complicated, but the following is a summary of its principal provisions.

1. A Land Commission was set up, and given wide powers to acquire land in advance of requirements, so that it could be available "at the right time". The Commission also received powers to manage land, and to sell or lease

land at full market value - or, if need be, on concessionary terms (Part II of the Act).

2.A Betterment Levy was imposed at a uniform rate - initially 40% of the development value - when land was sold, leased or realised by development. It was intended to increase this proportion later by stages. Liability for the Betterment Levy was subject to certain allowances, exceptions and exemptions. The money was collected by the Land Commission and paid into the Exchequer (Part III of the Act).

3.A new form of land tenure, Crown Freehold, was created, which was qualified by covenants reserving to the Commission future increases in values arising from development or redevelopment. Where a concessionary Crown Freehold was sold for housing, a covenant prevented the house owner from selling at a profit representing the difference between the market value and the concessionary value of his holding.

As with the Development Charge under the 1947 Act, liability for the Betterment Levy awaited action by the landowner. In this case it was the sale or lease of land, or the carrying out of "material development" - a term defined in Section 99(2) of the Act.

The added value which the owners expected to gain by developing, selling or leasing their "land" was termed the "net development value". This value was arrived at by deducting a complicated "basic value" (essentially, the current use value) from the market value. When this calculation revealed a realisable value, a "chargeable act" or event arose. "Chargeable acts" included the sale, lease or development of land; compensation for revocation of planning and other permission; grant or relief of an easement; and certain other "chargeable acts" designated by Ministerial Regulations.

Operation of the Act

A landowner became liable for "chargeable acts" arising after the first "appointed day", 6 April 1967. Thus there was a rush to start developments before the deadline. This often entailed digging holes or trenches, or laying foundations, as token evidence that development had started before the appointed day.

There followed uncertainty in the land market, which was reflected in the reluctance of landowners to part with their land. They might wait for a change in government and the abolition of the Betterment Levy. For owners of developable land, waiting was often no problem. Land, they observed, always increases in value in the long run. They had nothing to lose. Instead of more building land becoming available for development, there was less. The decline in supply tended to raise the price of what land was available. It was reasoned that since in many cases the retention of 60 percent of development value was not sufficient to make their land available, they would be still less likely to do so when the levy increased as planned.

Thus the objects of the Act were not being realised. Land was less, rather than more, readily available, and the proceeds of the levy fell far below that expected. Instead of the £80 millions expected in a full year, only £15 millions were raised in 1968-69 and in the following year only £31 millions.

Sir Henry Wells, Chairman of the Land Commission, came under fire, particularly from builders, who complained that land was not forthcoming as promised. According to the property correspondent of the *Observer* (December 1, 1968), Sir Henry had threatened to resign because of unfair criticism. "...I am tired of being nagged by builders. I am trying to help," he said, and blamed the planning authorities for not releasing more land.

During the life of the Labour Government of 1964-70, criticism of the Land Commission continued. It was labelled unjust, wasteful, and too complex to understand properly - even by professional advisors. And the Betterment Levy was self-defeating, in that realisation of its objects depended largely on action by landowners - whose interests were often better served by taking no action at all.

Repeal
The Land Commission and the Betterment Levy were eventually abolished by the Conservatives after they came to power in 1970. Subsequently a land hoarding tax, aimed at penalising people who had obtained planning permission for their land but had not proceeded with the development, was proposed, but came to nothing.

Then came the collapse of property prices, and many land speculators burned their fingers and were in serious straits.

Community Land Act 1975 and Development Land Tax Act 1976
Labour's third post-war attempt to regulate, control and manage land development and to collect development value for the community, took the

form of two linked but separate measures.

The first was the Community Land Act 1975, which had objects along the same lines as its predecessors: "to enable the community to control the development of land in accordance with its needs and priorities". The second was the Development Land Tax Act 1976, whose objects were the same as those of the Development Charge and the Betterment Levy: "to restore to the community the increase in value of land arising from its efforts".

The Community Land Act

This Act, which came into effect on 6 April 1976, was considered by many to be a half-way house to land nationalisation. Local authorities were given the power to acquire land for public ownership, by agreement or by compulsory purchase. The Secretary of State was empowered to dispense with a public enquiry as preliminary to a compulsory purchase order. Local authorities, having acquired land, had the responsibility of seeing that it was developed, either by themselves or by others.

The price to be paid was the market price, less any Development Land Tax (see below) payable by the owner. Thus the basis was current use value, which would exclude any "hope value" of the land being later developed for other purposes. The power of local authorities to acquire land became mandatory when a Duty Order was made by the Minister. The cost of buying land, including costs of administration and interest payments, etc., would be financed initially by borrowing, and would be repaid from the proceeds of disposals. Ultimately, purchases would be paid for directly by the proceeds of disposals.

Land for commercial and industrial development was to be made available on ground leases, of normally not more than 99 years. Land for residential purposes was to be disposed of either freehold, or by way of a building licence granted to the builder. Eventually the freehold would be conveyed to the house owner.

The Development Land Tax

The Act which introduced this tax came into effect in August 1976. Unlike the other Act, this was based on proposals for taxation of development gains which had first been made by the previous Conservative government.

The tax was to be administered by the Inland Revenue authorities, and operated in conjunction with Capital Gains Tax. It was charged on the realisation of development value. This could occur either by disposal of an interest or by "deemed disposal" on the carrying out of development. The tax was 80 per cent of the gains realised, except for allowances for low gains. It was intended that the rate should eventually be raised to 100 per cent.

The net development value to be taxed was the proceeds of disposal, less the highest of three basic values - a convoluted formula which roughly equated with current use value. There were exceptions, exemptions, allowances, conditions and special cases - all set out in 94 pages of explanatory notes containing examples, calculations and expositions to guide those who either had to deal with the Act or to advise others.

Criticisms of the two Acts

Conferences organised by professional bodies to explain and interpret the two Acts, and to conjecture how they would work, were held in several towns. Speakers and audiences alike were highly critical, revealing the uncertainty and frustration engendered by this land legislation.

Most of the criticism was levelled at the Community Land Act. The Conservatives promised to repeal it; but they were willing to go along with the Development Land Tax if it was nearer 60 per cent instead of 80 to 100 per cent.

Fate of the two Acts

The Community Land Act ran into difficulties after the Government's spending cuts of December 1976 reduced the borrowing capacity of local authorities by £70 millions. This severely restricted their acquisition of land, as there were no other funds available for the purpose. Meanwhile, pressure for repeal continued. A typical comment came from the President of the Incorporated Society of Valuers and Auctioneers: "Any suggestion that the Act should be retained and amended because the threat of repeal causes a greater level of uncertainty, should be opposed. A bad Act is a bad Act. A house of cards is no sounder because it has mosaic tiles on it." (*Estates Gazette*, 2 April 1977)

When the Conservatives came to power in 1979, they soon repealed the

Community Land Act and reduced the Development Land Tax to 60 per cent. The Development Land Tax was eventually repealed in the Finance Act 1985.

The reasons for failure

Post-war Governments, particularly Labour Governments, have repeatedly legislated with the object of making more land available for use, bringing down land prices, curbing speculative profits arising from the implementation of regional and national plans, enabling local authorities to acquire land cheaply and collecting for the community those land values which were created by the community. A great many people whose politics were not Labour have sympathised strongly with these objects.

Yet legislators who have attempted to deal with such problems have been unwilling to look beyond expedients like betterment levies, bureaucratic control of land use, and semi-nationalisation. Although the Acts were eventually abolished by political action, this was nothing more than the *coup de grace* to legislation which was manifestly not achieving the objects for which it was originally introduced.

The Acts failed for a variety of reasons. In the first place, they were complex pieces of legislation, and the more complex a law is the more likely it will be riddled with anomalies and unintended side-effects.

In the second place, there has been real confusion about what the word "land" means in different contexts, and people who sought to produce an effect on land in one sense of the word often in practice produced a completely different effect.

Thirdly, the legislators have been preoccupied with the speculative profits made by dealers and developers. This has led them to concentrate on capturing some of the gains which arise at the point of development and sale, or when planning permission is granted. Yet the current value of land at any time does not differ in any essential from subsequent increases in land value. The current value is merely the aggregate of increases which have accumulated since the time when land had no market value, and should not be treated differently from more recent increases. All that a betterment levy or similar expedient does is to tap the pool of land value at a point in time and to draw off a little; but in general it keeps the status quo.

Fourthly, there was no attempt to harness the self-interest of landowners.

Instead of inviting cooperation, the Acts provoked resistance or inertia.

Fifthly, the effect of the post-war land legislation on all three occasions (1947, 1965, 1976) was to deter development and the better use of land, to encourage land hoarding by owners and to produce an artificial scarcity of sites which were necessary for the creation of jobs and homes.

An effective and satisfactory way of achieving the essential objects which the three post-war Labour Governments all seem to have had in mind would have been to levy a tax on all land values - vacant land included, and regardless of its state of development. The value of different sites of land vary enormously according to a variety of factors which (unlike the value of improvements) have nothing to do with the activities of the landowner or his predecessors in title. These factors include fertility, the presence of minerals, ease of communications, proximity of towns, and the kinds of use permitted by planning and other environmental legislation. These factors would all be taken into account in assessing the tax. A full exposition of the theory and practice of land value taxation may be found elsewhere in this volume.

Sources and Bibliography

Board of Inland Revenue (1976) *Development Land Tax Bill. Explanatory Notes.*

HMSO. (1967) *Betterment Levy. Explanatory Memorandum on Part III of the Land Commission Act.*

HMSO. (1969) *Land Commission Betterment Levy Case Notes.*

Karslake, H. Howard. (1975) *The Community Land Act 1975.* Epsom, Surrey: The Land Institute.

Land & Liberty Issues for 1947-48, 1949-50, 1966-67, 1973-74, 1975-76. London: Land & Liberty Press, 177, Vauxhall Bridge Road, SW1V 1ER.

Pennance, F.G. (1967) *Housing, Town Planning and the Land Commission.* Hobart Paper No.40.

Ratcliff, John (1976) *Land Policy.* London: Hutchinson.

Postscript on Neo-classicism
Death rattle of a deadly paradigm
Fred Harrison

T hat economics as a social science is in crisis is now beyond doubt. Even leading exponents of neo-classical economics - the dominant paradigm - are expressing anxieties about the relevance of their theoretical apparatus.

> The extent to which such fundamental questions concerning mainstream economics are being raised by its leading practitioners is very striking. With such doubts about these hard-core issues, one begins to query the very substance of what is termed "neo-classical economics".[1]

The overriding characteristic of economics is its surreal quality, its *unworldliness*, the way in which it has been uprooted from its earthly origins. Nobel Laureate Wassily Leontief expressed it neatly:

> ...econometricians fit algebraic functions of all possible shapes to essentially the same sets of data without being able to advance, in any perceptible way, a systematic understanding of the structure and the operations of a real economic system.[2]

The competing schools of thought - Austrian, Post Keynesian, Marxian, Institutional - "are all afflicted with deep internal theoretical problems of their own". This is the assessment of one Cambridge economist, Geoffrey Hodgson,[3] who is acknowledged as a leading exponent of a fresh approach (evolutionary economics). Interestingly, however, while he concedes that Henry George's "intellectual influence was, of course, enormous",[4] Hodgson fails to incorporate into his appraisal of the chaotic state of economics the distinctive Georgist paradigm.

Existing paradigms have a proven track record of failure, and yet economists continue to struggle against new, real-world ideas. Why?

> This neo-classical monopoly in economics denies space and legitimacy for "all sorts of directions" and "all sorts of means". It provides a convenient mechanism for dealing with dissidents. Anyone who does not accept these core assumptions and methods is then regarded as simply not being an economist. It is not a question of whether they are right or wrong; those that disagree are simply sent into exile, into the sociology department or elsewhere.[5]

We should not now be astonished by this facility for suppression. For as Prof. Gaffney explains in *The Corruption of Economics*, a primary aim underpinning the original development of neo-classical economics was the ideological need to contain the influence of Henry George and his economic synthesis. That project is zealously perpetrated to this day.

> ...a crisis in the subject should not be taken to imply, however, that the orthodox or neo-classical paradigm is about to be overturned. The questions and controversies are so basic and important that the response is often to reassert belief in the fundamentals with renewed vigour, and to attack heresy with increasing force.[6]

Neo-classicism has reduced economics to an empty formalism. It no longer exists to study "a real object - the economy".[7] Hodgson notes:

> Of course, any science is likely to have a ruling paradigm and will sometimes eschew contesting approaches. But the point is whether the science is itself defined by the core theoretical elements of the ruling paradigm or by the real object of study.[8]

We can now explain how and why economics became sterilised from the real world, following the vibrant theoretical advances during the 19th century. Neo-classical theory developed with a private agenda: the need to detach economics from the politics that threatened the interests of the rent-seekers.

The device was an elegant one. Economics was transformed from science into metaphysics. If it was to succeed in its mission, it had to derive its substance not from external sources - the social logic of the real world - but from internal prejudices. Only by this means could it be used to neutralise the wisdom of political economy and deprive reformers of the language and tools that they needed to communicate rational policies through democratic dialogue.

The problem now is not so much the need to encourage economists to try harder: they will remain blinkered until they are embarrassed by the profound dissonance between their theories and trends in the real world. No; the primary challenge is the one that confronts citizens and their democratic representatives. For the need to develop realistic policies on issues like employment, poverty and inflation has to start with the determination to employ language that conforms to reality. That means we have to make a conscious choice, as I have argued at length elsewhere.[9] Do we wish the definitions of basic words in our language - words like "land" and "rent" - to be determined by a class ideology; or by the needs of the community?

Are we advancing a fanciful hypothesis? Our thesis is that key words in our language were hijacked by economists in the 1880s with the explicit intention of thwarting the aspirations of people who, by the million, had created a massive social movement in favour of the Georgist paradigm. Sceptics may wish to reflect on a parallel trend, documented by an Oxford University professor of English. John Carey has shown how intellectuals, alarmed by compulsory education for every child in the 1880s - which was perceived as a threat to their privileged role in society - reacted by making literature and art unintelligible, and therefore inaccessible, to the masses.[10]

But in the case of economics, it was not just the aesthetic senses that were blunted. The sinister dimension to the drama in the social sciences must now engage the energies of researchers for many years. For we have opened a box of dirty tricks that invites a new appraisal of the 20th century, which is likely to result in indictments in the court of public opinion. The conventional perception that we live in an age of social and scientific enlightenment is a hoax, the inevitable outcome of the stratagem against Henry George. For the hijacking of economics - the social science that was supposed to be concerned with meeting people's material needs - condemned us to a century of theoretical gobbledygook that matches the mysticism of the Schoolmen of the Middle Ages.

There is now no mystery about the source of the problem. To stop Henry George, they had to steal our language. By stealing our language, they stole our minds. By stealing our minds, they stole our lives. Melodramatic? Unfortunately, the mortality statistics bear out this diagnosis. Dr. George

Miller explains in *A Philosophy for a Fair Society* how welfare capitalism - the outgrowth of the policies of neo-classical economics, the system that was supposed to rescue capitalism from the stresses of social and economic crises - has betrayed millions of people. It allowed the driving economic force to lop years off people's lives.

But neo-classical solutions were doomed to failure because the fundamental cause of instability - land-led booms and slumps, one of the principal theses in Henry George's *Progress and Poverty* - was shrouded in mystery by the arch priests of neo-classicism![11] That, of course, was the object of the exercise.

The fight for the integrity of economics is literally a life-and-death struggle. The significance of that fact, for the evolution of society in the 21st century, is awesome.

References

1. Geoffrey M. Hodgson, *Economics and Evolution: Bringing Life Back into Economics*, Cambridge: Polity Press, 1993, p.4.
2. Wassily Leontief, Letter in *Science*, NO.217, July 9, 1982, p.107; cited in Hodgson, *op. cit.*, p.5.
3. *Ibid.*, p.7.
4. *Ibid.*, p.281, n.3.
5. *Ibid.*, pp.7-8.
6. *Ibid.*, p.6.
7. *Ibid.*, p.7.
8. *Ibid.*
9. Fred Harrison, "The Georgist Paradigm", in Mason Gaffney and Fred Harrison, *The Corruption of Economics*, London: CIT, 1994.
10 John Carey, *The Intellectuals and the Masses: Pride and Prejudice among the Literary Intelligentsia* 1880-1939, London: Faber and Faber, 1992.
11. Fred Harrison, *The Power in the Land*, London: Shepheard-Walwyn, 1983, and Mason Gaffney and Fred Harrison, *Land Speculation and the Business Cycle*, London: CIT, 1995.

About the Authors

V.H. BLUNDELL
Vic Blundell was Principal of the ESSRA School of Economic Studies in London for 25 years. He was Editor of *Land and Liberty*, the bi-monthly journal specialising in the economics and politics of land, and is author of *False Paths to Higher Wages* (1975).

FRED FOLDVARY, PhD
Fred Foldvary received his BA in economics from the University of California (Berkeley), and his PhD from George Mason University. He has taught economics in Latvia and the United States, and is the author of *The Soul of Liberty* and *Public Goods and Private Communities* (1994).

MASON GAFFNEY, PhD
Received his doctorate from the University of California (Berkeley). He is Professor of Economics, University of California (Riverside). He is Editor of *Extractive Resources and Taxation* (1967), and the author of an extensive list of studies on urban economics and public finance.

FRED HARRISON, MSc
Fred Harrison read Philosophy, Politics and Economics at the University of Oxford, and received his MSc from the University of London. In *The Power in the Land* (1983) he correctly predicted the global recession of 1992. Director, Centre for Incentive Taxation; Editor of the bi-monthly journal *Land and Liberty*. He is an advisor to Russian municipal governments and federal agencies on property and taxation reforms.

NICOLAUS TIDEMAN, PhD
Received his PhD from the University of Chicago. He was Assistant Professor of Economics at Harvard University (1969-73) and then Senior Staff Economist at the President's Council of Economic Advisers (1970-71), before moving to Virginia Polytechnic Institute & State University, where he is now Professor of Economics.

Index

Other books published by
Shepheard-Walwyn (Publishers) Ltd.
in association with the
Centre for Incentive Taxation Ltd.

Ronald Banks (1989)
Costing the Earth
ISBN 0 85683 111 5
Pb. £7.95

Richard Noyes (1991),
Now the Synthesis:
Capitalism, Socialism and the New Social Contract
ISBN 0 85683 124 7
Hdbk £17.95

R.V. Andelson (1991),
Commons without Tragedy
ISBN 0 85683 126 3
Hdbk £17.50

David Redfearn (1992)
Tolstoy:
Principles for a New World Order
ISBN 0 85683 134 4
Pb. £9.95

Books may be ordered through any bookshop,
or direct from
CIT Ltd.,
177 Vauxhall Bridge Road,
London SW1V 1EU.